The Diary of a SOLDIER

The *Diary* of a SOLDIER

Weathering the Storms of Life at All Cost, Through Blood, Pain, Sweat and Tears While Overcoming the Fears That May Linger Throughout the Years.

LYNNETTE JACKSON

WESTBOW
PRESS®
A DIVISION OF THOMAS NELSON
& ZONDERVAN

WestBow Press books may be ordered through booksellers or by contacting:

WestBow Press
A Division of Thomas Nelson & Zondervan
1663 Liberty Drive
Bloomington, IN 47403
www.westbowpress.com
1 (866) 928-1240

KJV: Scripture taken from the King James Version of the Bible.

ISBN: 978-1-9736-3355-6 (sc)
ISBN: 978-1-9736-3354-9 (e)

Print information available on the last page.

WestBow Press rev. date: 7/13/2018

DEDICATION

To My Late Husband:

MARVIN JACKSON
May 22, 1955 – March 23, 2017

DEAR READERS

Upon preparing to write this book, I had many obstacles and challenges to come my way towards this completion. Only through my faith, my trust, my belief and my dependency on the almighty God; was I able to succeed into making this book become into existence. Because I am a soldier in the army of the Lord and because I stand firmly as many others have gone on before me have stood boldly to do God's will; I carry out his message through my writings towards encouraging others to stand "on Christ the solid rock for all other ground is sinking sand." May you be inspired to put your best foot forward as you advance from this world of existence into the after-life!

Lynnette Jackson

CONTENTS

Dedication v
Dear Readers vii

CHAPTER 1   The Diary of a Soldier 1
1.   Power to Overcome the Enemy 1
2.   Live Love Laugh 6
3.   Run for Your Life 10
4.   Life is Worth Living 13
5.   Complete Your Assignment 16
6.   Don't be Caught Sleeping on the Job 21
Poem: Life Goes On 25
Poem: Cherish the Moment 27

CHAPTER 2   The Enemy's Territory 28
7.   Whose Side are We On? 28
8.   Stay Alert!! 33
9.   Is our soul right with God? 39
10.   S.O.S. --- HELP! HELP! HELP! 44
11.   Pick up the Pace 48
12.   Ceasefire 51
Poem: Wounded 54
Poem: Keep the Faith 55

CHAPTER 3   On the Battlefield 56
13.   Don't be Afraid of Death 56
14.   Keep it Moving – (On & Upward) 60

15. No Retreat No Surrender...64

16. How do we look in God's Eye's? 69

17. Don't Throw Your Life Away 72

18. Stop Rejecting God...75

Poem: Our Last Good – Bye..79

Poem: Mind Craft..80

CHAPTER 4 "On Your Feet Soldier"...............................81

19. Recess is over.. 81

20. Remember the Blood of Jesus 86

21. Just Stand... 91

22. Payday is coming after while 94

23. Make Time for God..98

24. Stand up and Vote for Jesus 104

Poem: Our Special Day 108

Poem: Thinking of You 109

CHAPTER 5 "Onward Christian Soldier"...................... 110

25. The Power of the Tongue.. 110

26. The Power of the Mind 114

27. The Power to Live by Faith 118

28. The Power of God's Love 123

29. The Power of Prayer 127

30. The Power of the Holy Ghost 131

Poem: No Turning Back... 135

Poem: Aftermath... 136

Poem: Today 137

Poem: There's got to be a God Somewhere.................... 138

Acknowledgments.. 139

CHAPTER 1

The Diary of a Soldier

POWER TO OVERCOME THE ENEMY

*O*ne may think that all one needs is to have courage and strength to subdue the enemy but; speaking the word of God will also defeat the devil as well as to have on the whole armour of God; which will protect us against the forces of evil that we may have to face along the way of our journey with the Lord.

Jesus was tempted by Satan in Matthew Chapter 4 and Jesus spoke the word of God to him three times and the devil departed from him. Jesus relied upon the word of God instead of fist fighting or cursing as his defense against the devil's attack.

We have the spirit of the living God that dwells on the inside of us to help us ward off Satan. And because we are of God, we have power to rebuke the enemy and anything that he throws our way in Jesus name.

God is our helper and our deliverer. We don't need to rely on a posse, a knife or a gun to defend ourselves. We must have faith in God that he will protect us in times of trouble.

Speaking the word of God in faith can move mountains and giants out of any situation because God can make a way out of no way for he will deliver on time.

That's why it is so important to know what the bible says because it is a lethal weapon. Knowledge is power and having the knowledge of God is within the pages of God's word. It is a road map that leads us away from the enemy mimes of the devil's obstacle course that has been set up to destroy us.

The word of God is not just to be studied to show others that we know the bible and its' contents backwards and forwards. Nor should it be studied just to acquire knowledge of saying that we know more than the next man or woman but, the knowledge of the word of God is to be shared to all by all so that all will know how to save themselves from the evil forces of this world.

We don't have to throw the book at each other to try to get someone's attention. But, we must know God's word for ourselves to be able to defend ourselves when the devil approaches us with his evil schemes and tactics.

We don't have to get all hot under the collar whenever someone hollers at us because, responding calmly and in a nice tone of voice often keeps anger from arising and allowing any mixed emotions to stir.

There are so many people who have lost their lives, jobs, or families because of them letting their anger take control and get the best of them by retaliating back in harsh words or actions. Falling to the trick of the enemy and playing right into his hands by them responding back without thinking or walking away from a situation.

When one doesn't give in to retaliation that does not always mean that one is scared or that one is weak. That just says that one is using their head and chooses not to escalate the problem at hand by possibly making matters worse if they choose to do otherwise.

There is power in the name of Jesus! So, in times of trouble; all that we have to do is to call on that precious name Jesus and the devil; as well as his evil informants will run because they tremble at the name of Jesus.

Yes! There is comfort in knowing that all we have to do is to resist the Devil and to rebuke him in Jesus' name and the devil will flee from us!

When someone hates us by slandering our name or causes us pain; we don't have to tell others about it. The flesh would love for us to strike back and do the same thing to them but; God does not want us to fight fire with fire.

God wants us to talk it over with him in prayer. God wants us to tell him all about our troubles through prayer because prayer changes things and having a little talk with Jesus makes everything alright!

We must turn everything over to Jesus by faith knowing that he will fight our battles for us and keep us safe from harm.

Therefore, we must not complain about the problem nor should we start confusion over the problem. Once we have given the problem to God; we must leave it there and let him take care of the rest.

In the meantime, we must stand still and let God's handiwork unfold. Jesus truly can work it out better than we can. Jesus has the master plan and there is nobody that can do it like he can.

We must keep the devil on the run by praying and fasting; pushing the power button on off to our cell phones, our television programs and start pushing back our meals sometimes for spiritual strength to defeat the enemy.

Praying and fasting helps in keeping our mind focused on the Lord and his plans for us. It also helps us to dedicate time to God daily and to receive spiritual nourishment; which empowers our spiritual mind.

True, we all need natural nourishment to have healthy bodily functions but some people let natural foods get the best of them instead of them controlling it. We are involved with spiritual warfare and Ephesians 6:12 says; "For we wrestle not against flesh and blood, but against principalities, against powers, against the rulers of the darkness of this world, against spiritual wickedness in high places."

We must not be so wrapped up in natural nourishment where we allow it to overtake us physically or mentally. If we would get full from God's word like we get full from our meals; our lives would be changed from the inside out. There must be balance and we must exercise the mind as well as the body for proper functions of the body.

The devil wants us to partake of things that will kill us. Satan is only out for himself because he doesn't care about us physically, mentally or emotionally. He simply hates us! The devil wants us all to burn with him in hell and it doesn't matter to Lucifer on how he uses us to help us to get there.

Jesus wants us to keep our mind on him which helps us to rise above distractions from the attractions of fine cuisines and buffets that are set before us. Jesus loves us and he is for us. Jesus wants us to have eternal life with him in the place that he went to prepare for his believers after this life is over.

We must pray and fast in order to last; for having the spirit of God on the inside of us will help us to be strong in the mind towards resisting the temptations of this world that overwhelms us to over indulge which can and will eventually destroy us if we don't fast.

We must arm ourselves likewise as Jesus did against Satan. Keeping on the whole armor of God and keeping our mind stayed on him; as we continue to seek God's guidance; helps us not to be tricked into taking sides with the enemy.

When we feel that nothing in our life is going right; we can praise our way through. There is also power in praise and it helps us to concentrate on the positive outcome of things. While knowing that the break through is on the way and that God will deliver us from whatever it is that wants to keep us down.

When praises go up; blessings come down. Just thank and praise God for everything, through everything and watch your miracle transpire. The devil can't do us any harm so sound the alarm from the rooftop by praising God for bringing you out. Lift up your head and your voices to let God's glory be revealed.

In closing, there is no shame in calling on Jesus' name; wherefore, we must remain steadfast and unmovable; abounding in the work of the Lord; until victory is proclaimed.

To live, to love and to laugh seems to be an everyday struggle for some people because with the way that things are in the world; all hope for some people seems to be lost and they feel that there is no need for them to do any of these three things.

However, these three things are a link towards survival that we all should include in our everyday lifestyle to help keep us sane and normal in this corrupt and confused society in which we all are a part of.

Furthermore, God wants us to live for he created us and God wants us to live among each other in peace and unity; and not with strife or hatred.

Why can't we all just get along and why shouldn't we all want to get along? There is something good inside of each of us for everything that God made is good and we must seek to do well to others and not do the evil that may come to our mind to do and to hate one another.

After – all, no one is more of value than the other person is; because we all are created equal and to live without all the chaos and confusion in this world could be possible but not without one having God in his or her life in order to be able to do so.

Living for God enhances the way that one lives their life because God is Lord over their life and he leads and guides them safely through this life. Therefore, one is dead to sin and now lives unto righteousness doing the things that are pleasing unto God and not the flesh.

While living for God; our thought patterns are consisted of the mind of Christ which allows us to be more love-able, more joyous and more peaceful towards one another as we live from day to day having the measurements of true concern and real love for others as well as ourselves.

We are more pleasing to God when we live in harmony with our sisters and brothers the way that God intends for us to do.

This world must come together as one and with God having dominion over our lives it can and will make that difference for change that this whole world needs.

But so many people are living for Satan who is the evil prince of this world and it causes the turmoil and the eruption and corruption of all of the damage that is continuing to go forth in this world today.

The devil is ruler over so many people in this world and they have the mind set of Satan which compels them to keep up confusion and division among other people around the nation.

With Satan being head of their lives; the darkness of hatred and bitterness fills their life by pulling them down and keeping them bound to their sinful ways of life without happiness or love from within; which carries hurt and pain to many individuals of this society in which we all are among.

Another key ingredient to living is to love. We also must love living which helps to add meaning to our life.

Now, who wants to continue to live in a world that's full of sin?

For only having the love of God within us can that truly make the difference of one truly wanting to love and to live in this life.

They say "love makes the world go round" but, Jesus gave us the ultimate meaning to love by him first loving us! Therefore, we must spread that love to others and this world is definitely in need of it.

Having God's love inside of us will flow freely to others which will help our love continue to grow.

There is joy and peace that comes with having God's love within; that one will want to share with others so that they too will feel complete all over.

We must let love show and glow in our lives by demonstrating it to others. If the whole world would observe and do this; the earth would be a better place in which we all would enjoy living on.

Now, what's a world without laughter?

We should make it a daily practice of thinking happy thoughts, doing happy things, being happy while living righteously and loving others wholeheartedly; laughing joyously.

After – all, there is a time to laugh and having a happy heart is like soothing ointment but to have a terrible spirit is a great disappointment. A little happiness goes a long ways especially when one has Jesus in his or her life. Besides, God does not want us to be sad or to be feeling down and out.

Having God in our life gives us that spark of life that we need to keep moving forward in life. For God will help us to lift our heart and our spirit through the days and nights that may trouble us. Therefore, we must not wallow in past mistakes, or live with regret and be in despair. Nor should we have self-pity of things that will pull us down and immobilize us.

God is all of the hope and the strength that we need to depend upon to help get us through each passing day. Meanwhile, we must never fear because; God is near and he will be with us every step of the way.

In closing, no matter what is going on around us or no matter what troubles may ail us; we must thank God for each new day that he allows each of us to see. We must keep choosing to live, to love and to laugh because God gave us life to live until his final appointed time of our demise from this earth and how we choose to adapt to this life while we are on this earth; will depend solely upon us.

In this day and time, we are living in a war zone and evil lurks all around us. How much does one value his or her life? Are we walking, skipping, lagging or perhaps dragging our feet through this life? There is no time to waste because our life depends on it. Safety is found in the arms of Jesus and we must run to him for our refuge.

So many people are running in the wrong direction which is leading them to the danger zone. So many people are running all around and are not paying attention to the warning sound and they are yet going down. We must run to the Savior like never before faster than ever because he only can save us from the calamity of this world.

There is a battle cry that's heard throughout the land and taking a stand to be on the Lord's side is our only demand. Jesus is our only help and he will help us but, we must run to him and he gladly will. "Run for your life!" "Run for your life!" Because our soul depends upon it!

When I was a child; I remember seeing a cartoon where this Chicken Little was running around saying: "The sky is falling!" "The sky is falling!" I laughed and I laughed because it looked so funny seeing the little chick running frantically around and nothing was happening.

I even saw a movie or two with the phrase saying: "Run for your life!" and the look of danger was all around and people were running here and there trying to take cover.

Today this phrase is no laughing matter and we all need to take heed to this saying concerning our life.

People are racing for the cure of a lot of diseases and the only cure to save us is to give our life to Jesus who is the only one who can cure us from sin. Therefore, we must run to this cure!

Jesus is the only cure for this sick and sinful world for after-all; being free from sin is the only thing that will truly save us in the end.

People run to and fro. Some run to work, some run to class, some run to the store, some run to get their hair and nails done, some run with the fellows and some people just simply run around here and there doing all kind of things but they won't run to God.

We must take life more serious and what is more serious than God? Nothing that we do; that is not relating to Christ is of more important than God. Gaining eternal life is of far more value than gaining material things that we will not be taking with us when we decay.

We must give our life to Jesus and we can't be afraid about what others may say concerning us giving our life to Christ or about us choosing to live righteously.

This world has become corrupt and we must want to flee from the dangers of it just as Lot and his daughter's did in Sodom and Gomorrah.

God is our refuge and he is our only guide safely to the other side after this life. Our life truly is in danger every second, every minute and every hour of each day because evil lies in wait all around and Satan wants each of us to be a part of his kingdom which is going down.

Satan, his empire, everyone and everything that's affiliated with the likes of the devil will be destroyed. Therefore, we must not give in to him and we must run to Jesus as fast as we can to make it to the safety zone.

There are too many distractions in this life and if we are not prayed up; we will get caught up in the tricks and trades of this life. Meanwhile, we must run to the arms of Jesus as Jacob ran from his brother, Esau who wanted to kill him for receiving the family blessing.

We must run for our life like David ran from King Saul who wanted to kill him because of his jealousy of him. We must run from sin as Joseph did run from Potiphar's wife wanting him to seduce her.

We must not be consumed by sin from doing wrong or by others wanting us to do wrong. We simply have a choice not to sin because we don't have to give into temptation whenever it comes our way or if it should enter our mind.

We should be strong in the mind and refuse to act upon wrongful thoughts. Jesus loves it when we stand up for what is right because we represent Christ as real warriors being strong in the Lord and in his power; we will continue to press forward doing what's right until his return for us.

In closing, no matter what we may have to face or go through in this life; we must continue to have faith knowing that God will surely be with us as we trust in him and keep his word. Therefore, we must continue to run with power and grace believing that God will take us through and deliver us safely from the snares of the enemy if we be willing and obedient to do his will.

Has there ever been a time in your life where you felt like nothing matters and you wondered why bother? Have you ever walked around in a daze or a trance and wondered what the use is?

Well I have and I am so glad that my way of thinking changed because; I really felt that just because things weren't going my way that truly my life wasn't worth living.

There may be some of you that have felt this way yourself; and others may even feel this way right now, today but, I have had a change of heart down through the years since then and God truly made that difference in my life to honestly know as well as to honestly say that life is worth living.

The fear of life to what lies ahead can stop us from wanting to continue on in life if we let it. Also, the fear of the unknown is not a joke but, we have to face our fears by taking one day at a time. Which means, that we can't be so rattled up about the mysteries of this life that it makes us want to exit this life.

How does one know what is at the end of the road if one never actually goes down that road to see for oneself? I am so thankful that I didn't let fear stop me or turn me around and go back in the other direction otherwise, I wouldn't be where I am today feeling optimistic about life and what God has for me after this life.

Because Jesus lives, he's the hope for brighter days. When one has Jesus in their life; there is no need to fear for there is no fear or failure in Jesus. We simply have everything we need to continue to live fearless each day in Jesus.

No matter what comes; we really can face tomorrow if it is to be a tomorrow because, Jesus holds the future and his love for us; let us know that life is worth living.

Life may not be a bowl of cherries and life may not be a ray of sunshine always but, we must take the bitter with the sweet and say: what will be will be and let it be because the world is in God's hands. God is fully aware of the things that's going on around us and God wants us to press our way and live.

Therefore, we must speak life to ourselves whenever we feel down and out over anything. Life is what we make of it for we have the power within ourselves to be happy or to be sad in this life because; it's through our attitude of how we accept things or how we pursue things in this life.

We must be so careful about what we say and how we say it. We must be so careful about what we think and how we think because, bad thoughts filter through our mind and it's so easy to act upon those thoughts especially when God is not a part of our lives. This is why it is so important for God to be the head of our lives so that he controls our lives as he leads and guides us safely through this life.

Life is a struggle everyday but having God in our life all day, every day makes life sweeter to manage because life is what we make of it and when we give love or show love; we eventually get love or be shown love.

God gives us the power to do a lot of things and with God as Lord over our life; the sky is the limit to what we can do and to what we can have in this life. Without God; we can do nothing and we could have nothing because, God made everything! God is life and love all wrapped into one and when we have God apart of our life; we then have everything that we need in this life because, God is everything!

There is no need to be down in despair for our God is everywhere and he is yet on the heavenly throne; so no, you are not alone!

We must not let Satan play with our mind by tricking us into thinking that we are worthless, useless or hopeless because, the devil is a liar and he wants us to lose hope but, Jesus is all the hope that we need and those who put their hope as well as their trust in the Lord; are blessed.

One can face anything in this life with God on their side. Living from day to day is more joyful and peaceful knowing that God is with you and that God is for you. This is even the more reason to want to keep living because, God won't let you fall.

In Closing, as long as God will wake us with a fresh new touch of his loving grace; we must be ready to run and stay in the race. As long as God allows the warm blood to continue to flow through our veins; we must continue to live every day for Christ so that we will forever reign.

We all have a task to do in this life and we must stay focused and get it done. We all are definitely here for a reason and it's to do the will of God. God never extends days beyond purpose towards carrying out his plans for us to do.

Therefore, God's plans for our life will be done before our time expires here on earth and through our life; others will see how they too, can be of help to someone else when one has the light of God in their life.

Then, God's will is being carried out through our life towards his assignment becoming complete by us telling others about Jesus; who is the Savior of the world.

Now, some people may not know how or where to start towards doing their assignment and some people may have a running start; while others may have a slow start but; if we ask God for his help and directions before we start each day; it's a beginning of a start towards doing God's will. After-all, we have to start somewhere and we must start somehow!

However, taking the first step isn't always easy but, it is the most important step towards completing any assignment and having faith and courage to do so is taking a grand stand in the right direction.

There is plenty of work yet to be done because, so many people still have not given their life to God. God can work through us if we allow him to guide us in ordering our steps along the way.

We must complete our assigned work and we must not be afraid to tell others about salvation and how Jesus saves! Although, Jesus has not come yet; Jesus is still coming back for the people who are saved from their sins and who believe on him.

People are dying and losing their soul; while giving up on life and are giving in to Satan and his followers because, some people feel that they have no other choice but to.

But, Jesus is the way out of any situation or dilemma that we may be in! We all have a choice to make to receive eternal life but, we must choose Christ and his way of living because, Jesus is the door keeper and the only way in is through him.

This important assignment that we must do; requires us to be strong in the Lord and in God's strength help to carry out God's plans by telling others about Jesus Christ and his love that he has for us all. Then, they too, will be able to know him and to experience God's love for themselves and will go boldly to tell others about the love of God; which now shines through them.

Therefore, this beautiful message of God's love will continue to spread like a wild forest fire and it will move towards others giving them hope for their soul to live for God; so that they will do God's will and fulfill their purpose to him in this life.

We are not here in existence on this earth just for our good looks and nor are we here to be catered to on hand and foot. But, we are here to help one another in doing the work of the Lord.

Meanwhile, no one should think or feel that they are better or more important than anyone else because, we all are created equal in the eyesight of God.

If we are reconciled to Christ; then we would have the love of God in us towards helping one another and with Christ in our life; we then become ambassadors for Christ which means that we will help others get to know Christ as well.

We are soldiers for God in his army carrying out a vital assignment and we won't be deterred by sitting down on God because, we stand boldly doing the work of God.

I Peter 2:9 says: "But ye are a chosen generation, a royal priesthood, an holy nation, a peculiar people; that ye should shew forth the praises of him who hath called you out of darkness into his marvelous light."

We are all one of God's children; chosen to help carry out his plan for our life. We don't have to take sides with the enemy and turn our back on God and fight against God. We are all chosen to stay on the winning team by staying with God.

The weight of this world is too much for us to handle alone but, God's way is light and he is always right there to lean on; while lending a hand to help carry our burdens or worries from the stress of this life.

The devil adds more and more drama to our situations which is like: "adding fuel to the fire." While, God will lift our burdens and he will even carry our troubles making life easier for us to bear when we are obedient to the will of God.

Thank God that we have a choice in life but, we must be willing to go through and complete our task to live eternally with God.

Meanwhile, we must keep working for God until our appointed time is over by God. We must not quit on God for he will deliver us on time and his time schedule is not our schedule. We must not attempt to clock out of this life; before our actual clock out time. God has much work for each of us to do and we must complete his will in each of our lives.

In John chapter 13; Jesus gave a great example of humility when he washed the feet of his disciples. He showed love and kindness to all 12 of them. Jesus has no respecter of persons for he went throughout, around and about doing good.

We as children of God are to exemplify Christ in our lives as well by showing love and kindness everywhere that we go to help draw others to Christ.

There are seven days in a week and 7 is the number of completion. Genesis 2:2 says: "And on the seventh day God ended his work which he had made; and he rested on the seventh from all his work which he had made."

This scripture tells us that even God completed his assignment that he set out to do and although he rested; it still was finished. So, rest if you must but don't stay away too long because it's hard for some people to get back to the task at hand if they let themselves get side-tracked or too comfortable to not want to finish what they've started.

Even the people in Joshua chapter 6 had an important task to do. Specific instructions were given and were to be followed through so that on the seventh day when they walked around the walls of Jericho seven times as the 7 priests sounded the 7 trumpets and at Joshua's command the people lifted up their voices; shouting for the Lord and the walls came tumbling down.

We all have victory in Jesus when we do what God wants and tells us to do. We can't push our project to the side and expect someone else to do it for us. We must keep moving until we are finished.

Jesus said in John 19:30, "It is finished." This is exactly what we all should focus on towards finishing up our course of being witnesses for Jesus Christ until he returns for us.

Jesus is the son of the living God and he left his heavenly throne from sitting at the right hand of the Father to serve humanity as well as to seek and to save all of us from a horrible fate by taking our place so that we wouldn't be lost from him forever.

Jesus is King of kings and Lord of Lords and he humbled himself by dying on the cross for all of our sins; completing his assignment to save us from sin. Now, all we have to do is to accept him and to acknowledge him for who he is; by believing in him for what he has already done for us.

In closing, there are a lot of hurting and wounded soldiers today in our mist who are in need of God's healing in the mind; as well as in the body. As soldiers, in the army of the Lord; we must have strength to administer a helping hand; so that others can stand and get back in the race to complete the assignment towards us all being able to stand together on one accord; having victory in the Lord.

Have you ever been so tired and sleepy that you could barely keep your eyes open? Well, I have and it was no laughing matter at all. One would do just about anything to be able to close those peepers for just a few minutes to get some ZZZ'S.

However, now is not the time to be sleeping on any job because; many things can happen while one is in dream land. Many things are at stake during the state of unconsciousness.

While sleeping on the job, not only can one lose their job but also; one could lose their limbs which could help to destroy one's lively hood here on earth and one could lose one's life not being attentive to what is going on around them and last but certainly not least; one could lose eternal life with God while not being productive for God.

Yes!! We all sleep and yes!! We all need some sleep to be able to function properly. God doesn't want us to sleep our life away and in Matthew 26:41 it says: "Watch and pray, that ye enter not into temptation: the spirit indeed is willing, but the flesh is weak.

We need to be alert and we need to stay alert in order to defeat the enemy because, he often attacks us in our dreams; while we are asleep. We need to stay in prayer with God to be able to ward off the attacks of Satan and only being in tune with God can we be made aware of any danger that is in wait for us up ahead.

Jesus was in prayer with his Father on the Mt. of Gethsemane and Jesus had to receive strength through prayer to face his enemies who were in route to kill him.

If Jesus would have been sleeping; he would possibly have been weak, vulnerable and tempted to not die on the cross for us and we would have all been destroyed forever. But, thank God for his loving and caring sacrifice that he made for us.

The sins of the whole world was at stake and Jesus took our place when he died and he shed his blood on the cross for you and for me.

Jesus gave himself as a sacrifice for humanity and he defeated the devil's evil plans to condemn and to destroy us all. OH! What a price Jesus paid for us!

In spite of the pain and the shame that Jesus endured for us; he refused to sleep because Jesus had his mind on doing the will of his Father and he had his eyes on mankind towards saving us from an eternal death of burning in hell.

Jesus chose to take our beatings and our scars upon himself so that we wouldn't have to. Jesus spared our lives and he took the fall of dying for us all. Yes! Jesus died and he rose from the sleep of death!

I Corinthians 15:55 says: "O' death, where is thy sting? O' grave, where is thy victory?"

We cannot and we should not close our eyes from the truth which stares us in the face each day of God's love that he has for us. Therefore, we must not continue to choose to sleep on doing the work of the Lord by running away from him.

We must choose to be saved from our sins and go to tell others about the Savior of the world who is alive and well; for Jesus is yet saving those who will believe and who will receive him.

In Matthew 26:40 it says: "And he cometh unto the disciples and findeth them asleep, and saith unto Peter, what, could ye not watch with me one hour?"

Jesus simply caught all of his disciples sleeping on the job and all they were to do was to stay awake and to pray while Jesus prayed.

Staying awake can sometimes be hard to do and some people go through many extremes trying to do so for instance: some people drink coffee or caffeine sodas while others try energy base drinks or No doze pills to help them to stay awake.

However, our body is not designed for us to stay awake all of the time and proper rest as well as proper sleep is needed which helps us to be revitalized and rejuvenated from day to day.

Also, we must not have a desire to want to sleep all of the time either because it can make one become lazy, weak and unproductive concerning one's life. Besides, there is more to life than to just sleep it away.

There is much work to be done because a lot of lost souls has yet to be reached and we must continue to try and help them to get to know Jesus. Which by the way, the lost souls can't be reached if we are laying down on the job.

We must get busy and stay sharp on our feet; doing the work of the Lord with no retreat until the Lord's return.

The enemy wants to catch us off guard because he wishes to sift us as wheat and to devour our soul. We can't afford to get caught in the devil's trap. We must remain watchful and prayerful because no one knows when God will return.

The bible says in Matthew 24:44 – "Therefore, be ye also ready: for in such an hour as ye think not the son of man cometh."

We can't take this saying lightly because, Jesus said it and it will come to pass. We must be ready when Jesus comes. We don't have time to play around while dibbling and dabbling with our soul.

We can't ignore the signs of the times and think that Jesus is not coming back for his chosen people. We must be living for Christ and we must be in right standards with Christ.

In Closing, we must keep doing God's will. There is no time to be tipping out on God because he will come quickly!

SOLDIERS: "Be READY and ALERT"

SOLDIERS: "KNOW THEM that LABOR AMONG YOU"

SOLDIERS: "BEWARE of the ENEMY"

SOLDIERS: "BEWARE of your SURROUNDINGS"

SOLDIERS: "DON'T let your GUARDS DOWN"

SOLDIERS: "LEAVE NO SOLDIER BEHIND"

SOLDIERS: "BE ye STEADFAST and UNMOVEABLE"

SOLDIERS: "MOVE OUT!!"

The days seem so strange
Without me hearing you call my name.
Shattered and scattered pieces of my heart
Fall to the ground without a sound.
Wondering what the new day will bring
Now that you are not around.

Nobody but God will ever really know
How much I truly adored you and loved you so.
I had flown so high above the sky like never before
As my life with you had just begun to soar.
OH Yes! My love, we were a perfect score!

Now I know that life will never be the same
And all the memories of you in my mind and in my heart
Will only remain.

Thank you for sharing a beautiful love with me that I
Never felt nor knew; that was so strong, genuine
And yet forever true.

But, don't fret my love; I won't turn back
Nor will I let go of what I held that was so precious
And so dear; just know that soon one day
I will be near.

My life will go on because I know that I am not alone.
I have the man himself from up above
Who will forever comfort me and shield me
With his undying love for me.

Although our life together here on this earth is no more;
We truly were a perfect score!
And as I continue to travel to-and-fro
Near are far with a scar
Life goes on
Until I too; will be called home!!

Where is the gleam in the eye and the sparkle to the smile that
once razzle dazzled as it shown? Will it ever spark again?
Where is the shine and the glow that used to naturally flow
Will it ever show again?
Life is but as a vapor for it too; comes and goes
Cherish the moment!

For as we sometimes walk around in a daze
from the haze of this life's maze
Trying desperately to figure out how and why
Cherish each moment!

Know that love lives on through the hearts
of others as one passes it along
Therefore, please be strong and live on
Cherish this moment!

Then the beam of the sunlight will one day break
through to you and take away the dampness from the
chill in the air that tried to cause you despair.
Now the twinkle in the eye and the brightness of
that radiant smile has shown through again
Cherish your moment!

CHAPTER 2

The Enemy's Territory

*I*n the world today in which we live; there are many teams to choose from concerning the sports industry and everyone seems to want to be on the winning team but of course, some choose the under dogs because as we know it; there's almost always one team that's considered as the losing team.

Now, just as we may choose in life of who we vote for, who we may choose to mingle with or to who we may choose to ride with. We must be like Joshua and choose who we are going to serve; whether it's God, the devil or man.

When one chooses to be on the Lord side then one is definitely on the winning team for one can't lose while having God on their side because, there is no failure in God.

Unfortunately, I have just burst someone's bubble when I mentioned this question concerning whose side we are on because, I am no longer talking about sports. Now, I am simply asking are we for God or are we for the Devil? Are we for doing what's right or are we about doing what's wrong? Are we striving to make it into heaven or are we gliding our way into hell? Whose side are we really on? Because, we definitely can't straddle the fence towards rooting for them both!

If we are not fulfilling the scriptures of God's holy word; then we are not on the same page with God and therefore, we are against God by not being on board with God and his plans.

When one does the ways and the will of Satan, then one is on the enemy's territory which goes against the ways and the will of God. One can't do and one won't do that which is pleasing to God while one is serving and siding with the Devil. Nor will one whose affiliating with the things that are of the Devil; be approving of those who choose to please God.

God wants us to be holy just as he is holy. Therefore, the only way that we can be holy is by having him in our life for his guidance towards helping us to live righteously just as he is righteous.

Making a decision to be on God's side may cause one to become separated as well as to be isolated from family members and friends because; jealousy and hatred often seeps in.

Now, that one has become a member of God's family and have disengaged from the Devil's family; Satan doesn't like it and he often causes trouble to arise and to be in the midst of things by causing confusion; which wars against the people of God.

Therefore, inquiring minds would want to know whose side are we really on these days? We all must check our lifestyle by how we live our life each day; or by what we do each day in order to have a clear and definite answer to the question for ourselves.

Who or what is #1 in our life? Who or what is the source of our life? Who or what controls our Life? If God is not the answer to all (3) of the questions mentioned above or If God is not at the top of our chart of being the head of our life then something or someone else has our under divided attention and our affection which clearly states whose side we are on; and that's the Devil's territory!

"God is a jealous God." Therefore, we must not place anyone or anything before him. God wants us to choose him, his plans and his love over anything that the enemy has to offer that tries to captivate our minds to follow him which leads us out of the safety zone of God.

We must not get relaxed during our mission for God and become sided tracked for any reason by anything that Satan or that this world tries to entice us with.

True, we all may have wandered into unfamiliar territory at one point and time or another in our life span and we may have felt a little uncomfortable as well as out of place once we got there but; just because it may look decent or seem OK that doesn't mean that it always is.

Satan sets up traps and snares to make believe that everything is fine and dandy but, once one gets farther and farther along they become comfortable and familiar to the surrounding of it all that they began to fit in, to join and to settle in with the enemy.

We can't be holding hands with the enemy as if we are skipping along daisies. This road that we are treading on is like a mine field and we must not play on the Devil's territory of being deceived by his lame games that he plays to kill, to steal and to destroy us in.

Meanwhile, we must keep our guards up at all times and only when we are led by God will our guards stay up. And therefore, we will have no need to fear the enemy because we are on God's side. There is plenty of peace and comfort while being on God's side as one goes through the dangers of this life being pursued by the enemy.

We have nothing to worry about or nothing to fret over when God has our back and Just as God was there in the old testament days for the children of Israel; God is here today for his people who love and obey him because, God is yet a present help in times of trouble and we must believe and depend upon him to see us through.

One should be tired of the roller coaster rides that they are on; while siding and riding with the devil. Being up today and down the next day; in spirit, in finances and in relationships having temperamental changes with the ways of the world – love/hate, happy/sad being filled with agony and turmoil day/night captured by the ways of sin. To state it plainly; there is no peace of mind or rest to the wicked.

Satan wants us to live our life in continuous misery day-in / day-out, week-to-week, month -to- month, year after year, from sun up to sun down; wearing a frown and sad as a clown. The devil shows no mercy to anyone.

Who should want to keep living their life this way?

"Misery loves company" that's what they say and some people want to see others living their lives this way just so they won't live this way alone.

God has something better to offer his people and only when one turns to God will one then experience true happiness of real joy, real love and real peace because, only God gives this satisfaction in this sinful world that we all live in.

Therefore, we must run to the arms of Jesus for his protection that guides us safely through on this battle ground.

Victory is only found in Jesus and corruption as well as destruction is the passageway of Satan.

We must not be misled into saying that old cliché "If you can't beat em' join them".

We must refuse to be blinded by the trick of the devil of thinking that having fame, fortune, power, success and pleasures of this world is the key to life, love and liberty because only Jesus saves and can provide the true happiness that one longs for.

One must not be deceived into thinking that life here on earth is forever because it's not and there is much more in store for the ones who truly believe in God and who are on his side when he returns for his true followers.

The devil is hell bound and all of his followers will join him in hell if they choose to stay connected to him.

One must look at the bigger picture up ahead by choosing life over death. God's gateway leads to eternal life and the devil's pathway leads to eternal damnation.

So, whose side are you on? For only God and you know the answer.

One doesn't have to be bribed to be on God's side. For either one will do what's right or one will do what's wrong. It's that simple!

In closing, we must examine ourselves as we count up the cost of what we value the most towards us truly knowing whose side we are really on.

There is so much unseen forces of evil throughout this world that we can't always see; and getting in tack and staying tuned with God is the key to subdue the blows that Satan often throws our way to get us off course. I often sit and wonder about the people of long ago and I ponder on the things that have happened over the centuries of time past; knowing that God was with them in the midst of their troubles and knowing that God is yet with us during our time of trouble as well; and staying alert under all circumstances is very important towards defeating our enemies in this day and age.

Just as God gave instructions then for his people to stay on the right path that he chose for them to go; so that they could receive the blessings of the Lord; we must obey God as well to reap the benefits of our blessings from the Lord. God is our road map to having eternal life and strict instructions are required so that we won't be side tracked to turn away and go in another direction; which will lead us down the wrong path away from God.

Therefore, we must stay in the presence of God by praying and fasting as well as meditating on his word; to be led by routes in which to take; while being on this journey with the Lord. There are too many distractions in this world today in which we all have our own mind towards doing our own things. We must be real and we must get serious about the things that matters the most in this life; concerning our life.

Some people invest so much time in doing worldly things and getting worldly possessions letting precious time pass them by; while investing in any and everything but the most important things; which is time that's invested doing the will of God and time that's spent in the presence of God.

Some people have time to do just about anything that they would like to do. Some have the means to travel just about to anywhere that they would like to travel, some have money to practically throw away towards buying just about anything that they would like to buy while disregarding the price; living life as if they own the world; forgetting about the one who made the world.

God wants our time and our attention so that we will do his will and not to do our will of doing our own things. Just as God walked and talked with Adam, Moses, Abraham and many of the prophets; God longs to walk and to talk with us daily as he leads and guides us in the path of his righteousness.

But, many of us are walking to the beat of our own drum and are drifting farther and farther away from God and his righteousness by our own actions and distractions of this life.

Complaints and anger from our surroundings often arise but, we can't let it get the best of us and cause us to sin. For, in Numbers Chapter 20; Moses disobeyed God and out of anger of the people; he hit the rock twice instead of only speaking to the rock as he was instructed by God to do; his actions caused him to miss out on crossing over into the Promised Land.

In the book of Genesis, Eve was distracted by the words spoken to her from the serpent. Then, Adam became distracted by Eve (his Wife), while partaking of the forbidden fruit that he did eat. Which then caused them both to be put out of the Garden of Eden because of sin from their action of disobedience to God.

Those that know God; know his voice and they will follow him to wherever he leads them. We must discern God's voice and the true leading of God from the trickery and the sneaky voice of Satan and his false dealings. People today, get off course by listening to others or doing things with others that are not of God. Which then causes them to have great distractions that leads them to a destructive lifestyle away from God.

God's leading will never steer us to do wrong nor will it lead us in the wrong direction because he loves us and everything that he does for us is for our good. God wants to keep us safe from our enemies and we will avoid the traps and the snares of our enemies when we listen to God as we walk and talk with God.

Having a day-to-day personal relationship with God will keep one on the right path of God. Therefore, one must not be deceived by everything that look's good or that sounds good because it may not always be what it seems to be. In other words we must not believe everything that one says.

In the meantime, one must get connected to God and stay connected to God for safe guidance of not being led away and astray from God. We must know the word of God for ourselves and we must obey the word of God for his directions as well as his instructions concerning his plans for our life.

Just as a seed is planted in the soil to grow; we too, must have God's word planted in our heart to know and to grow more spiritually in him so that we will not fall away from him.

There are a lot of spiritually blinded people in today's society that are isolated from God unaware because, spiritual blindness deters one from seeing clearly the proper things that are truly of God which could help them to stay on the strait and narrow path to God.

One must not be hypnotized by the material things or the worldly things which causes one to lose sight of God. Meanwhile, we must keep our eyes on Jesus and look to him instead of looking back and longing for things of time-past as Lot's wife did in the 19th Chapter of Genesis.

Having sin in one's life doing hateful and disruptive things that the devil loves; will cause one to miss out on receiving God's eternal reward that he has in store for them in the end if one doesn't repent of their sin; by asking for God' forgiveness.

Therefore, we must not fall to the likeness of sin and nor should we give in to sin by letting Satan have control over our life.

Sodom and Gomorrah was completely destroyed because of the sinful people and this world as we know it too; will one day be destroyed because of the sin that's steady being committed throughout the world.

Only the true believers that stand with God now; will reign with God in the end if they continue to withstand the test and trials of this world by holding on to God's hand and by doing his plan.

Knowing that no matter what this world may try to advertise; that it's no comparison to what God has prepared for them in heaven. I Corinthians 2:9 says; "But as it is written, Eye hath not seen, nor ear heard, neither have entered into the heart of man, the things which God hath prepared for them that love him."

Because no one knows the mind of God; therefore, we can only imagine what heaven looks like. We should look forward to seeing heaven one day by being prepared for God's arrival and by being ready as well as staying alert; towards doing God's will so that we won't miss out.

Looking to be a part of God's kingdom and his righteousness should be first and foremost in our lives. We must not let anything keep us from putting God first in our life because nothing or no one is more important than God and nothing or no one is worth the risk of losing one's soul to the pit of hell, and being forever separated from God.

Once one realize the seriousness of God's wrath; then one will recognize the importance of reorganizing one's life by submitting to God; the giver of life.

Philippians 4:8 says; "Finally, brethern, whatsoever things are true, whatsoever things are honest, whatsoever things are just, whatsoever things are pure, whatsoever things are lovely, whatsoever things are of a good report; if there be any virtue, and if there be any praise, think on these things."

We can't let our mind be entrapped by negative and unpleasant things that weigh us down and keep us down; by the unseen forces of evil in this world. Therefore, staying focused on God and his word will keep our mind perfectly maintained.

When we meditate or concentrate on God and his righteousness; it steers and veers our mind in his direction; away from the dis-pleasurable things of this world. If we put God's words into practice and keep it in our heart; as well as in our mind; it will help us not to do sinful things that will displease him.

Knowing God's word for oneself helps to defeat the enemy as well as to not be deceived by false doctrines; that are being delivered through false prophets. Not only should one know the word of God; but one should obey the word of God; for it is very vital towards one staying on the path of God; while being spiritually lead by God.

Therefore, we must not fool ourselves by just hearing the word of God being preached to us but; we must also apply the word of God to our lives and do what the word says.

Just as the children of Israel were guided by the pillar of cloud by day and the pillar of fire by night during their journey in the wilderness; we have the bible- (God's Holy Word) to guide us and to help us stay on the battlefield; which also gives the assurance of God's presence with us while being within us; during our continued walk with him.

Just as a soldier must stay alert and be prepared for the enemy's attack; we too, must be alert and prepared to defend ourselves by relying on the word of God. Furthermore, we must not continue to walk spiritual blinded to the things of this world by continuing to be misguided, misused and abused from the lies told by the unwise.

We must not be deceived by Satan or his conniving people that he has chosen to try to dissuade God's people from following Christ.

Therefore, trusting and believing in God gives one the will power to lean on God and to walk out of darkness into the light which leads them to Jesus Christ; (the Savior of the world).

Jesus suffered for the sins of the world and he died on the cross for you and I. (The sinners of the world). He then rose from the grave having victory over death which paved the way for all to have victory over sin; as he made the way; for all to get to heaven and make it in.

We must keep the faith and fight for our life by pushing through any obstacles that tries to hinder us from getting to our Lord and Savior; Jesus Christ.

In closing, there is a crown of righteousness waiting to be received by those who have stayed on the path of righteousness and have believed.

The first thing that comes to mind to some people concerning this question asked; is probably followed with a question: what is a soul? The soul is the immortal part of the body that will live forever after death. The earthly body will die and go back to it's original form as dust. But the soul will never die and where our soul will live; only God will reveal.

Our soul returns to the Lord once we die and God has the final reply where it will lie. How one chooses to live their life here on this earth is very vital towards the outcome of one's destination once one leaves their existence of this world. Once one has passed away and just before the close of the celebrated day; the familiar quote: "ashes to ashes and dust to dust" is usually said because, the humanly existence is no more.

God made man from the dust of the earth and gave him life and man became a living soul; hand crafted by God. Man is nothing without God. For we are all God's creation and we wouldn't be a part of this world's existence had we not been a part of God's plan to include man.

Our soul and everything that we have and everything that we are is because of God. He "beautifully and wonderfully" made us in his image for his purpose to do his divine plan. But, some people have literally sold their soul to the devil and they are doing the devil's plan instead; which displeases God.

Our gifts and our talents were given to us by God which are to be administered for the glory and the honor of God and his purpose; and not to bring show and praises of honor to ourselves.

However; fame, fortune, power and success have swollen the mind of many people by Satan; towards them thinking that they are invincible which then leads one to think more highly than one should of oneself; as one falls into Satan's control while doing his plans losing focus of his own soul.

What is it going to benefit us by gaining this world? What are we trying to prove to this world? Or, what will we do to win the world's approval of us and lose our soul in the process of trying to do so?

We must not boast and brag about our God given gifts and talents because as easily as they were given to us; they can be easily taken from us.

To God be the glory for all the things that he has done for us should be the thinking mentality of all mankind for the goodness of God.

Therefore, we must not be deceived by our riches, our cars, our homes, our jobs or our status quo.

No medals that we may have received, no badges of gratification, no stars of fame bearing our names are going to help any of us on the Day of Judgment that will be granted by God.

For these are only accolades that too many pride themselves of and absolutely nothing of this world that we have here on this earth will matter to God on our day of demise.

We will not be taking any of our accumulations of worldly possessions, nor our claim of fame with us to our eternal destination. Because only our soul will then matter; for only our soul will remain.

Living for Satan is simply not worth the risk of losing our soul when it is all said and done in the end; that so many have already chosen to do.

Our soul will live eternally either in heaven or in hell and our lifestyle plays a major role towards where that will be.

So, instead of choosing foolishly to do the things that's pleasing to the devil which will only guarantee that the soul live miserably forever with Satan; choose wisely to do the things that are more pleasing to God for assurance of the soul living forever peacefully with God and having a personal relationship with God daily helps towards our soul being right with God.

When one has personal fellowship with God; then one's soul will not crave for worldly things which are not of God because; their soul will crave for spiritual things as well as spiritual food and spiritual water which will nurture and satisfy the hunger as well as the thirst for God that will help one to stay connected to God.

The soul yearns and thirst for God; just like the whole world needs God.

Like a flower needs the sunlight and the rain to help it grow; the soul needs the nurturing of God's love and with God's love residing in us; we'll have love to share with others.

As we choose to follow Jesus; our soul can rest in Jesus and the devil can't do our soul any harm because, it is safe and secure from all alarm. Therefore, we must not be afraid of Satan for any reason because; we can call upon the name of Jesus and he will come to the rescue to deliver us.

Oh! How refreshing it is to know that God loves us so; and that our soul can rest safely in Jesus' caress. Even in the face of death, we need not fear for Jesus is still near and our soul is yet anchored in him.

God does not want us to walk around living in fear of one another; though man may hurt us but, man nor the devil can destroy our soul. Meanwhile, we shouldn't be afraid to live for the Lord.

We all will cross the path of death one day, for the word of God says; "be ye also ready." And making preparations now by asking for God's forgiveness of our sins while we yet have life in our earthly bodies; will determine where our soul will reside once we die.

So many people, are living for so many other things other than for the Lord; while yet being concerned about things that are not important and are spending excess time thinking about getting ahead in life.

This world is not our home. And this world as we know it to be; will one day pass away because, we are not here to stay.

Living for the Lord is the best decision that anyone can possibly make to be able to spend eternity with him.

Until one makes this important decision to follow God; their soul will constantly wrestle from confusion in the world and the lack of inner peace that only God provides.

The soul searches just as one tosses and turn in bed from a restless night of sleep that is much needed or perhaps, like Jacob wrestling with the angel all night and dislocated his joint (thigh) for wanting to be blessed by him.

We all long for something in this world in which we live in; craving for satisfaction that only God can give.

Like a deer that searches in need of water to drink; it soon will find the water it seeks. Just as our soul searches in need of the living God; we too, will find the peace of God, as we seek God.

As we dedicate ourselves to the Lord; we must concentrate and meditate on the Lord; loving him with all of our heart, with all of our soul and with all of our mind. So that we will find: the mysteries and the wonders of his love; from up above.

Psalm 84:2 says;" My soul longeth, yea even fainteth for the courts of the Lord: my heart and my flesh crieth out for the living God."

Our soul should be shouting for joy, giving reference to God for being God of all creation. As we thank God for his love, his grace and his mercy that he shows to us daily. For we should never forget who we are or whose we are.

In closing, we are valuable to God and God wants us to spend valuable time getting to know him by being in the presence of him; with a song in our heart.

SAVE OUR SOUL!
S.O.S. Is a distress signal and immediate response is needed.

I've often seen television programs where people were stranded on an island from shipwrecks to airplane crashes and the familiar (3) letters S.O.S. were imprinted in the sand; in desperate hopes that someone would come to their rescue.

Today, there are Coast Guards as well as Search and Rescue teams to hopefully recover those who may be in dire need of them.

However, we may not have been lost at sea or stranded on far away land but we may have felt lost and all alone under different circumstances which may have made us feel helpless, hopeless, scared and frustrated because help seemed to be nowhere in sight.

I imagine that John - (the disciple of Jesus), may have felt many mixed emotions when he was exiled on the Island of Patmos by Roman Soldiers because of his witness about Jesus Christ.

Those who are now witnessing for Jesus Christ today; find themselves in similar situations of being isolated from perhaps certain family members, peers, neighbors, co-workers and the world in general for standing up for God's righteousness and they are hated by the devil and his followers.

But, one must not panic or be in fear because just as God was with John on that deserted island; God is yet with his people and they can call on him for help during anytime and God will hear them.

The bible lets us know; that God will never leave us nor will he forsake us and that's the assurance that God is forever with us no matter where we are.

There were many frightening dilemmas mentioned in the bible where only God could deliver them from the hands of their enemies. Such as in:

1. Daniel 6:16 – Daniel was thrown into the lion's den for praying to God.
2. Daniel 3:21 -- The (3) Hebrew boys were cast into the fiery furnace for not bowing down to King Nebuchadnezzar's golden image that he had set up.
3. Mark 4:37 – The disciples were out to sea during a great storm trying to get to the other side.
4. Jonah 1:17 – Jonah was in the belly of a whale (3) days and (3) nights for being disobedient to God.

Wow!! How terrifying this all must have been. Especially, to be swallowed whole by a great big fish.

If ever they needed help; this was it!

S.O.S. was definitely in demand and only God could have intervened for their safety.

All of these incidents were terrifying situations to be in; but God performed a miracle to each of their lives which brought them out victoriously.

Just as the people of God went through many trials and tribulations for God back in the bible days; we too, must endure whatever the task may be to stand for God during these last and evil days of our trying times.

Knowing that God is with us and that God is for us should help to see us through our hardships.

Therefore, we must not run away from God and make things worse for ourselves. For we are to trust wholeheartedly while depending on our Lord and Savior; Jesus Christ no matter what the problem may be that one may face because Jesus will be in the midst of it all.

Just as the troops fight for victory during a war to get back home safely to their loved ones; we too, must "fight the good fight" of faith in hopes of having eternal victory with Jesus in heaven when he returns.

Meanwhile, all of our hope is in Jesus and when we ask for his help; things began to change because calling on the name of the Lord truly makes the difference in our lives.

Just as when we ask for something we expect to get it; when we look for things we hope to find whatever we are looking for and when we knock on a door we wait for someone to answer and open it.

There is nothing wrong with asking for help because we all need help sometimes in this life whether we may want it or not.

God wants to help us but, so many people let their pride get in the way of them asking for help which sometimes gets them further into trouble by trying to fix things themselves. Pride can lead to a great fall of things and we should never let our pride get in the way of us calling on Jesus' name because, everything that we possess is because of Jesus. The Lord giveth and the Lord taketh away; then we'd have nothing.

For as long as we live, we are always going to need Jesus and his help whether we want to admit it or not. God is in control of everything because he created the world and everything that's in the world.

We are God's people and he wants us to call on him by praying to him with a humble heart and spirit. Being obedient to him and subject to his will for he will forgive us and make everything alright for us; if we repent and turn back to him for his help.

Therefore, we must let go of pride and lay our burdens aside; fall down on bended knee so God will hear our plea.

In closing, God is the only one who can save our soul during this sinful generation in which we live in. No matter how things may seem; God is the source through which all of our blessings flow. We are never alone and all hope is not gone if we remain strong because, God is on his throne.

There are moments in our lives when it seems that time just flies by. Then, there seems to be days where time seems to move so slowly. But, the truth to the matter of it all is that there are 24 hours in a day; and the days, months and years come and go like the seasons all change. We must keep moving in spite of what is going on around us and know with each day that God grants us; the new day is in motion whether we like it or not. Meanwhile, we should get up and get busy towards telling someone about God's goodness because, someone; somewhere didn't wake up to see the new day.

There is no time to sit around feeling sorry for ourselves or dreading that the new day has begun. We may not be ready to face the new day but, know within our heart that whatever it is that wants to keep us in the state of sadness or loneliness that God will see us through the struggles of it all; if we are willing and able to take the first step because, God will be right there beside us every step of the way as we follow it through.

We are to be like soldiers in the service who carry out orders from their commanding officers. As disciples of Jesus Christ, we all have been given the great commission to carry out his good news of the gospel to others who are in need of getting to know him.

But, how are we to go out and about to tell others the good news of Jesus Christ if we have stopped along the way? How are we to spread the good news or to carry out God's plan by lagging and dragging our feet? We must continue to keep our focus and our stride going as we scurry to hurry towards making his mission complete. Keeping a steady pace to run this race for God will determine our victory in the end.

But, however, we often get side tracked by looking at things on the daily news or to the latest social media apps that are programmed to our screened devices. In the mean-time, we must not let anything come between us towards getting through the finish line to Jesus. Therefore, we must keep our eyes on the Savior as we put more pep in our steps and keep moving in his direction.

We must be like the Apostle Paul and hold tight to our faith in Jesus Christ; so that we may receive eternal life. In order for us to hear God say well done thy good and faithful servant; it is going to take total determination on our behalf as well as perseverance to make it safely to the other side to be with God in the end.

Therefore, we must not half-step during this course. The devil is on our heels and we can best believe that he's not playing with us about it. Satan wants to trip us up and to see us fall on every angle because the devil simply doesn't care about any one of us. We must stay ahead of the enemy by keeping our eyes on Jesus Christ at all times because looking back is not an option.

Don't worry about the steps that you take or how many steps that is being made; just keep stepping. One doesn't even have to use the pedometer to keep track of the steps taken daily for God; just keep stepping. Our steps are instructed by God and God has us covered when we do what is pleasing to him as we keep walking in his direction; God will take care of us.

Meanwhile, we must not break our stride under any circumstances because; evil lurks on every side and Satan is out to destroy. Just as a commander tells his platoon to charge into battle against the allies; we too, are to charge into battle for the Lord as we stand up against the enemy forces of this world.

The children of Israel had to charge into battle many times against their enemies and as long as they trusted and obeyed God; victory was theirs. There is no need for any of us to stand in fear of our enemies because, just as God was with the Israelite then.... God is with us now and we are to move by faith proclaiming the victory.

We all as individuals play a very important part towards having victory in our life and that part is for us to have faith. With faith the impossible can take place because, faith can move mountains in our life.

To have victory, one must proclaim victory; for faith without works is dead!

Therefore, one must move by faith in their walk with God to be able to receive their just reward from God in the end.

This war that we are in isn't over yet and we must proceed in telling many others along the way that Jesus saves, that Jesus heals, that Jesus delivers, that Jesus restores, that Jesus refreshes and that Jesus refills. There is hope and victory in Jesus and we must proclaim his name until victory is won!

In closing, God will order our steps towards him and all we need to do is to keep placing one foot in front of the other in his direction; as he leads and guides us safely to our eternal destination.

There is entirely too much killing going on in our nation today which shows the lack of respect for life that God gave to each of us. God will take care of the situation consisting of the injustice that is being carried out in this society. Meanwhile, we do not have to try and be God because, we can rest assure that he will handle all vengeance according to how he sees fit to do so.

God is the giver of life. Therefore, one must not take matters into their own hands by destroying life. For we are to love our sisters and brothers as we live in peace among them and not hate them. But, the world is filled with sin and there is very little or hardly any love left in the heart of men. And, the world is yet dividing more and more by violence with the lack of compassion for one another because of so much sin from hate and jealousy that's in the world.

However, having hatred or jealousy towards others is not the answer. Love is; for it erases and melts away any bitterness that one may have towards another. Therefore, we have no reason to continue to hate or to continue to be jealous of anyone because, we are to have love one to another by spreading God's love to all mankind.

There is excessive blood that's been shed and like the song sang by: Mandisa which says; "we all bleed the same" that is so true and yes!! Jesus experienced it first hand for all of man; by shedding his blood on the cross for the sins of the whole world.

Jesus gave his life for our life and paid the ransom of sin to join us all back together again in the end.

Therefore, we must stop the madness of hurting our fellowman with lies and words of hatred that cut like a knife. And, we must stop killing one another with the rage of jealousy from the blow of the fist or from the shots fired of a gun and hold up the blood stained banner of Jesus

Christ; God's only son. As we stand united with each other in love, peace and harmony shouting Ceasefire!!

God is all that this world needs because God is love and if one has God in their life; he supplies the love that helps one to share with others.

Therefore, we must reach out to our brothers and sisters who are in need by sharing the love of giving hope, time, food, clothing, shelter, conversation, smiles, hugs and money because, when one does this to the least one of them; it was done unto the Lord as well.

God knows all and he sees all that we do; meanwhile, we must do all things to the glory and the honor of God.

One can't enter into God's kingdom which is surrounded with love; if one has no love for their fellowman; because their heart, mind and their soul is filled with sin from within.

One must not continue to let Satan take control of their thoughts into thinking that they can change the world by eliminating, hating and discriminating against anyone. We must live together here on this earth in order to be able to live together in heaven. Therefore, we must not give in to sin and let the devil win.

There's a lot of controversy today over this and over that but, we must not worry because prayer changes things. Putting things in God's hands for him to work out is the best thing that we can do. Turning it over to the Lord helps us to keep our sanity. There is no need for any of God's people to run around in despair and pull out their hair for God is in control and he is their defense.

God knows the outcome of everything and turning things over to him is much better than one trying to fix things themselves. Meanwhile, we must not worry about things that we can't change or things that we have no control of.

The battle that so many of us are trying to fight belongs to God and just as God was there to deliver the children of Israel out of the hands of Pharaoh during the crossing of the Red Sea; God will make a way for us as well if we let him.

The devil loves to stir up confusion among the people of this world and if one doesn't have their mind on God to see them through things; one could lose their mind and do wrong things. We must not be so quick to get mad where it controls us emotionally that we want to become disruptive and unruly.

Losing one's temper and blowing one's top can be disastrous; for we often do things at the spare of the moment by leaping into action instead of thinking about the consequences of our actions once the damage is done. Ceasefire!!

Staying focused on God keeps one calm through any storm that comes. When we take our problems to God in prayer and leave them there; God will quieten the storms and give us peace that we seek that only he can give to us.

It's not easy trying to live in this world with so much ciaos and with so much hatred among men with different views but, we all should try to work towards making a change within ourselves to help spread God's love, God's joy and God's peace to all mankind to bring unity among us; which begins by accepting Jesus in our life to make the difference of how we treat one another in this life.

In closing, the day will come when, "the wolf and the lamb shall feed together" but until the Son of Man appears; we all must share this world together as we strive to stay alive.

Silent tears fall like rain
As quiet as a driven snow
They flow.

But as I dry my eyes I sigh
Because the time flew by
As I thought of how and why
Our love vaporized
Unto the skies.

I miss the US we were
For only God truly know
The love we shared was not just for show
For it was genuine and pure as a fallen snow

As each day comes and goes
I am given help and strength to carry on
Knowing that I too have a date
And I won't be late
For I will see you again at the appointed time

Then
Theses silent tears will be no more
For all sorrow and pain will cease
Now only joy and happiness will be released
And I too will finally be at peace!

Gazing across the majestic skies
Watching God's creation as it flies.
Oh, the wonders and the glory of; his precious love
That's oh, so beautiful and oh, so pure; as a gentle dove.

The world often seems so distant and so cold
As chilling secrets of old; gently unfold
From the revealing truth of the things untold
Which drives one to stand up; to be brave and to be bold.

No more whispers, no more pain
For there is sunshine after the rain.
Victory is on the other side
Just sift through the ashes and arise.

God is yet with us through it all
Whether it's big or whether it's small
Or
Perhaps, if things may began to fall
Keep the faith
And lift up your head and stand tall!

CHAPTER 3

On the Battlefield

DON'T BE AFRAID OF DEATH

*W*e all are going to cross paths with death because there is no way we can avoid death and there is no way we can we run or hide from death. For, we know not how, when or where death will take place but, knowing that it will come someday; helps us cope with the inevitable. However, we must not be afraid to die and nor should we be worried. Especially, if our soul is right with God because, God will help guide us to make the transition safely through to the other side. So, sit back and enjoy the ride while holding on to the hand of God.

There is a time for everything and since we all have been born; we all have to die. So, just as life began here on this earth for us; it too, will end for us one day.

God doesn't want us to spend our time on wondering how or when we will die but, he wants us to spend the time that he does give us by helping to win souls for Christ so that when their time should come in passing from this life here on earth; that they too; will be able to then live forever with him.

As Saints of God; there is joy in knowing that we then will die in the natural body but we will be raised in the spiritual body. The comforting part concerning these words is that after we have passed away; we will then be in God's presence.

Those who have died believing on the Lord Jesus Christ; will finally be resting in the Lord away from all harm on this earth until Jesus returns. I Corinthians 15:55 says; "O death, where is thy sting? O grave, where is thy victory?"

All of God's believers have nothing to fear about death because, the dead in Christ will rise again and we all will happily rejoice together again; forever with the Lord.

Death didn't hold Jesus from being resurrected from the grave for on the third day; Jesus rose with all power from the grave having victory over death and that same power now lives in his true believers. God's power will then quicken our mortal body to rise up to meet him when he returns for us.

Each new day that is given to us should be cherished and used wisely as if it were our last by doing the things that will be beneficial towards the kingdom of God to help lost souls get to know God.

Murmuring and complaining, fussing and fighting, bickering and hollering at one another is a waste of precious time. Therefore, we must turn all the negative energy into positive energy to be utilized towards loving and helping others to have hope in God.

Therefore, we must stay focused in this life and look for ways to live peacefully with our brothers and sisters here on earth until our time should come as we bow out gracefully when our name is called home.

Meanwhile, there is plenty of work to be done and souls are yet to be won. God is still waiting for his people to repent of their sins and the devil is yet reeling the sinners in his direction. In the meantime, the saints of God must keep witnessing to the lost so that they too; can die in Christ and live again.

Death is not the ending but, it's the beginning of life for those who have died in Christ and who have been faithful unto the Lord until death. For, the dead in Christ will live again forever with the Lord.

Now, this should be great music to everyone's ears and this news must be shouted from the rooftops so that the whole world can hear that all have a chance to have true victory by standing on God's side holding up the blood stained banner of Jesus Christ until victory is won.

Death is a transitioning from one existence into another therefore, a true believer in Christ doesn't sit around focusing on dying because death has no power over believers who die in Christ.

Philippians 1:21 says; "For me to live is Christ and to die is gain."

God must be the subject of our life whether we live or whether we die because, having God in our life guarantees victory over death with having life with Christ after death. This is a win-win situation to all Saints that have died with Christ in their life.

Having faith in God gives us hope towards living with God after this earthly body puts us down. Placing our future in God's hands is the only assurance of man having a winning chance of making it into heaven.

If we don't have God a part of our life while here on this earth; we will not be a part of God's life after this earth passes away.

We must wake up and look around us because death is in the land and it surrounds us. Some people are literally playing with the devil by robbing, stealing, fussing, fighting, smoking, drinking, lying, fornicating, gambling, selling drugs, selling their bodies and the list goes on and on as one continues to play Russian Roulette with his or her life.

Romans 6:23 says; "For the wages of sin is death; but the gift of God is eternal life through Jesus Christ our Lord.

We must not continue to think that we can live forever doing these things that are displeasing to God. Jesus is yet watching us and he is yet knocking at the door of our heart for us to let him come into our heart and to change our lives for our good.

The devil is yet laughing at us because, we are playing right into his hands while doing his plans. And, we are yet falling farther and farther away from God as we draw closer and closer to our destruction.

Therefore, we must not let the devil win by continuing to sin. We must fight for our lives as we run for our lives away from the evil that wants to consume us.

God is a present help in time of need and he will save us if we will only call on him and look to him for his help. We can't change on our own but, God can help us to make the changes that we need help in; that we are attached to if we will only ask for his help.

In Closing, look to the light of Jesus and he will lead and guide us safely through our dark stages and phases of this life; into the afterlife.

With the way of the world today with all of the tragedies, disasters, earthquakes, hurricanes, tornadoes, mudslides, deaths and with life's extras; how does one tolerate such calamities or why would one want to keep living under such stressful conditions? Well, times were terrible in biblical days and just as people of long ago had to pray and to keep the faith to endure; we too, must strive to survive and stay alive knowing that God is by our side; makes it all worthwhile as we keep in stride.

Even when things fail or people may seem to come against us; we should praise our way through the mishaps and stay encouraged in the Lord; knowing that God can and that God will give us strength to push through any of life's distractions that tries to keep us down and hold us bound. Giving up on life isn't an option! We must know in our heart and know in our mind that God is with us and that he won't put more on us than we can handle. In the meantime, we must gird up our loins and keep it moving towards God.

Therefore, we must not let anything stop us from getting to our eternal destination to be with the Lord. Because, we must keep moving in God's direction to reach our goal and to receive our eternal reward that God will give to us; when he returns for us.

We must not be like the children of Israel always complaining which could cause us to miss out on entering into heaven. For, we should be grateful to receive any of God's blessings and be obedient to God's word by witnessing to others about Christ so that they too, will become witnesses for Christ; and they will help lead others to Christ as well.

We have plenty of work to do that will help us to keep moving for Christ. Therefore, we are driven by the spirit of God to be like the prophets of old that moved by the hand of God; towards changing their situations.

We, as Saints of God; are to pray for deliverance in the lives of people everywhere who don't know God. Prayer works and it changes things. Therefore, we can't stop being productive in life just because things may seem negative about life. We must pray and believe God by faith; for the impossible things to take place in this life.

Lives are changed through prayer; and prayer indeed is what this whole world needs. However, many people feel that praying is a waste of their time and won't pray at all. While some people don't believe that their prayers are being answered because they haven't received the results that they expected. Then, they doubt God and they give up on God which makes their situation worse than it was before.

We must keep the love of God moving in our lives; by passing love through prayer into the lives of others. Therefore, we must pray for our enemies in spite of; and let God be God; as he takes care of the rest while doing what he does best.

God's love is powerful for it can woo and win the heart of every man, woman, boy and girl to change this entire world.

Therefore, we must keep moving until a change has come. Consistency is the key towards being a winner for God. We can't let life's challenges discourage us from doing the work that God has commissioned us to do.

The little shepherd boy David; didn't let the giant Goliath; nor his size intimidate him from getting victory over him; and neither should we let anything take our focus off of our victory that God has for us when we keep pushing through our obstacles to get to him.

Though things may seem out of control at times and nothing that we do seems to work; we must stay focused and know that God is yet working behind the scene of things and that God is working it out according to his plans for our life.

For instance, in Joshua Chapter 6 when the Israelites compassed the city of Jericho; they had to carry out strict instructions given by God for seven days and the walls of Jericho came tumbling down.

When we have total faith and total trust in God; it can move mountains in our lives that only God can remove. Therefore, the enemy hasn't got a chance to stop a man, or a woman; who is in the will of God that's living a life for God.

God isn't going to let anything come against those who aim to please him.

God is forever with us; just as he was with the children of Israel through there rebellion and disobedience; God is yet with us as a faithful friend until the end.

Meanwhile, there is no need to fear the enemy. Only keep the faith and believe in God above because, it's through God giving us the will power to succeed that we can achieve. But, we must keep moving for God in the direction of God; for he will never leave us nor will he forsake us on this journey with him.

God can and God will deliver us safely through the quirks and the perks of the maze from this world that we live in.

Having a made up mind as we walk by faith will help us to endure this journey as we continue to run this race with the Lord.

God is with us every step of the way; through the twist and turns or the ups and downs that we may face in this life. But we must keep moving in God's direction no matter what.

We also, can't dwell too long in the past for it wraps us, as it traps us; from looking to what lies ahead. Therefore, we must keep in sync by keeping in step; while keeping our eyes on Jesus who is "the author and the finisher of our faith;" who enhances us to reach that heavenly place.

Yes! Losing a spouse, losing a parent, losing a sibling, losing a child, losing an aunt or uncle, cousin or special friend may leave us feeling lost, disoriented, stagnant and confused but if we hold on to God; we won't lose.

Death is just a portal of moving from one existence into the next existence. For, just as day and night still go forth; we too, must continue to go forth until our end of the road has come to its life's end. And yes! God will be there with us even then.

Just as Jesus was faithful even until death of enduring the cross; we must be determined to live for Jesus at all cost. Jesus gave his life for us and he kept moving to do the will of his Father on our behalf. Now, we too, must keep moving in his direction to do the will of our Father in heaven as well.

In the meantime, we must depend on the strength from God to help carry us through our heartache and our heartbreak. And, let God wake us and guide us back into life; ready to fight.

In Closing, life is full of disappointments and uncertainties in this world but, there is one thing that we can be certain of and that's having eternal life in heaven; if we choose to keep moving with full devotion in God's direction to finally meet victoriously; the holy God.

Have you ever felt as though your back was up against the wall or that the world was closing in around you; as all hope seemed to be gone? Have you ever wanted to give up because you felt that you had no other choice but to; or perhaps that you were fighting a losing battle? God is bigger than any problem that we may have to face in this world. Therefore, we must not fear and become overwhelmed with things in this life. We must let the power of God from within us; lead and guide us safely through our everyday endeavors. For God's spirit that is within us is far greater than anything that exist here on this earth that challenges us.

God will give us the strength that we need to endure anything because, with God all things are possible. Therefore, we must not retreat nor should we surrender to the enemy; for defeat over the enemy is accomplished through knowing Jesus Christ.

A true soldier for God will withstand any obstacle that is placed before them; by looking ahead at the bigger picture towards their victory. We must stay focused to our task at hand and push through to reach our heavenly destination. Meanwhile, all negativity is pushed aside as we strive to stay alive while being on this timely journey with the Lord. So, in between-time, rest if you must; but don't retreat and don't surrender!

Thank God, that Jesus didn't retreat from his selfless mission to save us from our sins. Meanwhile, we should never give up on our Savior for his undying love that he gives to us daily.

True, our earthly body will give out and get tired from this earthly labor but, we must not give up and give out and retire on spreading God's word to others that are in dire need of him. We must continue to be an example of Christ to others; so, that they won't give up or give in to staying with Christ.

As long as we have breath in our body, God still can use us to do his will. Moses was 120 years old and Joshua was 110 years old when they died but, they didn't let their age stop them from doing God's will and yet still; did a faithful service for God all the way up until God called them home to glory.

Therefore, we can't let nothing stop us from being the great example of Christ to others because, the lives of others rest upon the pillars of our faith.

Furthermore, the strong survivors are a true blessing in disguise through the eyes of the weak. So, we must not retreat nor should we throw in the towel; others are watching through our lifestyle.

Thank God, for the wise words of the old because, all it takes is one word from God that's given to the old that can help to save a soul from the error of their ways while being entrapped by the enemy.

Therefore, we can't stop telling others about Jesus Christ; the son of the living God. We must continue to tell of Jesus' love and his forgiveness to the rich, the poor, the sick, the lame, the young, the old, the black, the white, the sinner and the saint. No, we can't stop our mission for God until we are out of commission from our earthly existence.

I hear the song which says; "Go tell it on the mountain over the hills and every- where, go tell it on the mountain that Jesus Christ is born." We have plenty of work that is yet to be done so that souls can be won for Christ.

Meanwhile, we can't get too comfortable by putting our feet up and retreating on doing our work for the Lord. We haven't heard God say; "well done thy good and faithful servant" until our life is done here on earth from mankind.

For only, those that have done God's will and who are faithful to him until death will be able to hear those words. So, we must stay on the battlefield and keep fighting for the Lord.

Therefore, we must not retreat and we must not surrender to the enemy nor his enforcers that tries to hinder us from leading others to Christ. Only through obtaining a close and personal relationship with the Lord daily will help us to keep moving faithfully for the Lord.

In the meantime, we must keep talking to the Lord in prayer. We also must read and study God's holy word, we must pray for others, witness to others, encourage one another to stand strong for God and fellowship with others for we are helpers one to another building our faith in the Lord.

In Judges Chapter 7, Gideon had a total of 300 men that went into battle against their enemies and they won the victory with God's help. They didn't retreat nor did they surrender during their battle with their enemies that out- numbered them tremendously.

This let us know clearly that it does not matter how big the task maybe that when God is with you and when God is for you; how can you lose?

We don't have to fear because, God is near. Therefore, giving up is not an option!

We must simply be willing to see the task through and God will provide an opening for us to keep passing through until that task is accomplished in our life.

Only trust God and believe that the impossible will be achieved; then, praise God and receive joy and peace because we have been relieved.

However, our earthly mission to continue to follow God and to tell others about God isn't officially over until God releases us of our earthly task once the last breath in our earthly body is grasped. Therefore, we must not wave the white flag nor should we through in the towel and quit witnessing to others about Jesus Christ or their salvation because; there are still many lost souls that are yet to be won for the Lord.

The Saints of God are valuable as well as important to God by doing the will of God. We must lift up our voice and let it ring as we sing; to tell the world about the risen King. Our voice is important and all it takes is one voice to create a declaration that can help to save a nation. The Apostle Peter is a prime example in Acts Chapter 2; as he preached to the crowd to repent of their sins and to be baptized in the name of Jesus Christ and 3,000 souls became new believers of Christ.

Therefore, we must continue in our journey and never stop preaching and teaching towards spreading the good news to others; about Jesus Christ. For it is God that we must serve and not man. However, we do a service for God in telling others about God because we are servants for God.

In the meantime, and in between- time, we must not lose our love for God or others while being on our mission for the Lord. Because, this race that we are on isn't just about us saving ourselves; we must be concerned about salvation for the souls of others as well. So, we must run and tell about the Savior of the world as we endure our task for the Lord until the end.

In Ecclesiastes 9:11 it says; "that the race is not to the swift, nor the battle to the strong"- Meanwhile, we must stay focused on God and depend on God as we do the Great Commission to keep witnessing to lost souls in hope that they will repent of their sins so that they too will be victorious with Jesus in the end.

It does not matter who we are nor does it matter about how long that we may have professed to have served God; this battle for God isn't over until God says that it's over. Therefore, we must be faithful unto God; in doing the will of God; until death.

We must be determined to stay on the battlefield for the Lord no matter what kind of storm may come our way to hinder the process towards us getting our victory in the Lord.

God can use anyone of any age to get what he desires to be accomplished in our lives. In the meantime, we must not make excuses and re-neg on doing what God expects us to continue to do for his purpose; towards helping the people in this fallen world to receive Salvation.

Meanwhile, we must not lay our weapons down neither should we play around. For, we must keep on the whole armour of God at all times while staying in the race for God; as we fight by faith to continue to overcome the enemy of this world.

In closing, we must band together as one and we must stand together as one. While being united together in love; until we ascend together in heaven above.

People have become obsessed with the way that one may look and with the way that one may dress which causes a lot of distress in today's society. However, it is perfectly OK to look different and to dress different in this world. Because, God made us all different in some way or another. And, even identical twins have some type of difference or preference somewhere and that's OK too. Because, God loves us all and it's all about how God looks at us that really matters and not about how others may look at us.

Therefore, we must not let things get us down because our face isn't on the front cover of a magazine nor, should we let it tear us down because we can't fit into a pair of designer jeans. We should not wig out or stress out because of what the world thinks or says about us. From this world's point of view, we all fit into different categories such as:

The Lower class, the Middle class, or the Upper class. We are the Have or the Have not. We're considered as Black, White or Mixed. We're told that we are pretty, fair or ugly. We're called out as fat, skinny or medium and the list goes on and on.

However, we should not let words of discrimination alarm us; nor harm us in this life because, none of us are better than the other; for we all are equal in the sight of God.

Furthermore, it still doesn't matter about the expensive clothes that we may possess; we should thank God for simply having clothes to wear. It does not matter about what hair color or hair style that we may profile; we should be thanking God for the hair that we may or may not have. And, it does not matter if we are a particular weight or a particular shape, color or size; we must be thankful to God that we are alive.

How God describes or defines us is really all that matters because, we all are "beautifully and wonderfully made" in the image of God and everything that he does is good. How God see's each of us is far more important than how this world see's us because, God see's us in all of our varied forms as he looks into our heart; which is displayed on the inside of us that the world can't see.

For what's in the heart; comes out of the heart and we all need inner beauty which will show how beautiful we really are. True beauty begins inside and it is revealed on the outside of us. Therefore, when God's love shines through us; the genuine beauty of our inward attitude will show love, respect and kindness to others that all will be able to see on the outside of us.

When we have that inner beauty of assurance within ourselves then we won't be disturbed by non-acceptance of others through their negative views of control to dominate our lives by trying to change us or to make us fit into this world's making of us. Having God in our life will give us the true happiness in our life; to help us to withstand the bitterness, the hatefulness and the ugliness that this world displays towards us.

God's approval of us is the only approval that we need in this life. God loves us even if some people in this world may not. However, that is no reason to come unglued or to run and hide from the people of this world. Because, once we learn to love ourselves and to accept ourselves as well and to see ourselves as God see's us; then negativity of any sort won't be entertained with harmful actions of any kind that would like to arise within ourselves.

Other people's opinion will no longer matter concerning oneself being of less importance in this world. For, we are all somebody special in the eyes of God and we should be treated equal whether we do or whether we do not have things of value. Because, we all are valuable to God whether one believes it or not.

There's a saying that says; "Small things come in great packages." What may seem small and simple to one person could often mean a lot to another person. For, it's the small and the simple things in life that we should value and cherish the most.

We will never be able to fully satisfy some people's mentality of us but when we learn to accept that we are only human and when we do our best and when we give our best with what God has blessed us to be able to do and to give of ourselves; then we can be happy with only God's acceptance of us.

Furthermore, If we all focused more on God and what he sees in us instead of focusing on what this world see's in us then; there could be less hurt displayed in the world of jealousy or pride and far less suicide.

No one should feel persuaded or forced to a level where they feel that they are not wanted in this world or that they are not good enough to live in the world that they would want to even think about ending their life or to take a life from this world.

We must stop the madness and come to our senses and just accept who we are as a person by getting Jesus in our life and letting God make the changes of our life to help make the difference in this life.

Let's start by spreading the beauty of God's love that's within us; towards others who are around us; that will flow to others and surround us all into a full circle of love that can remain with us for life.

In closing, a pure ray of loveliness is what God's eyes will see. For, we will finally be perfect and made the same; bearing Jesus' name. Then, each of us will finally see; how we truly look to thee. For, each of us will look and be holy as he.

Life is precious and it can be taken from us in a blinking of the eye. So many people take their life for granted and they don't seem to care whether they live or whether they die. God gave us life and what we do with our life is very important to God. Therefore, we must be thankful to God and live in a descent manner among mankind realizing, that every day given to us is a precious gift from God.

Many times, people do dangerous things just because they think that they can or perhaps, for the thrill of it and the rush of fun they want to experience from it. This is indeed considered living dangerously, ("life on the edge") as a dare – devil would choose to live. However, we must not tempt our fate by playing dangerously or by living loosely with our life for, life could be gone from us in an instant.

Therefore, we must not take life for granted because we are not invincible and nor are we replaceable. Some people live their life on the edge as though to be looking for trouble. Living life on the edge; is like jumping out of an airplane high in the sky; without a parachute. Some things that we do to ourselves can't be reversed. Meanwhile, we must think before we leap by thinking about the consequences of our actions before it is too late. Because, we don't always get a second chance to make the wrongs that we do in our life right.

We must make good use of our life and the things that God has blessed us with. The saying, "waste not want not" comes to my mind and I think about Jesus making mention in the bible; the parable of the lost son in Luke Chapter 15. The younger son received his inheritance from his father and left home to go live his life the way that he wanted to and he wasted his substances foolishly.

We too, can hit rock bottom in life by choosing to live carelessly. It does not matter how much abundance that we may have because, we can lose it all in a split second if we don't manage what we have wisely. Which goes to say; that we can lose our life or our lively hood as well; if we don't take the time out to think logically, plan properly or to take our life more seriously.

Many people today, boast and brag about their life and the material things that they have in this life as well. But, what they fail to realize is that they wouldn't have any of it without the help of the Lord. For, without God we all would fail.

Can one imagine, how Samson must have felt in Judges Chapter 16; when all of his strength that God gave to him; left him after his seven locks of hair was shaved off his head.

It shouldn't take us loosing something to realize how important it really was or to notice how good we may have had it. However, this is normally what happens before some people "wake up and smell the coffee" or they "never miss the water until the well runs dry."

We simply must value our life by living for God; to be more pleasing to God which; will then help us to show more appreciation to God for our life. When we live for God and not for ourselves, then, we realize how important our life really is to God; as well as to others, by doing the will of God.

There is great potential in each of us and God do not want us to be careless and to live foolishly in this world by living recklessly concerning the things that we do with our life. We should want to live our life as an example of Jesus Christ to be a blessing towards this younger generation; so that they too, would want to live their life for Christ and become great examples for others to follow after.

Therefore, we must not be deceived by the devil; into thinking that there is not going to be a penalty that we will pay for smoking, drinking, gambling, doing drugs, clubbing and fornicating every day. One must not continue to live his or her life this way.

For, one is wasting their life away as their body and soul deteriorates from the damage of sin that's being done.

In the meantime, we must focus on doing those things which are more acceptable to God and which will benefit us towards being a faithful follower of Christ.

God does not want us to harm our bodies nor does God want us to harm ourselves by living our life any kind of way. "We reap what we sow" in our life. So, the choices that we make concerning our life should be greatly pondered upon.

However, we can choose to let God order our steps and we can take the path that he places before us to be safe in his care. Or, we can choose to go our own route and do our own thing which takes us out of God's safety zone.

We also must humble ourselves before the Lord in prayer and ask God for his guidance to what we should do daily; then, we will have respect for God, man and our self-concerning; how we must live in this life.

Therefore, we must look to God towards living a purposeful, enjoyable and full life. With God's help of self-control as we crucify our flesh daily so that we may live by God's standard way of living instead of our own standard way of living.

In closing, if we live humbly before the Lord and have God as the head of our life; he will give us the meaning and the fullness of this life by providing his highlights to our life; that's full of his love, his joy and his peace that will last throughout our life.

All throughout the bible; we read about or we hear about; how many disastrous things took place because of sin. Sin has continued to fill the heart and mind of man; which is yet destroying one another throughout the world by the greediness and the selfishness of man wanting to have more power over this world; that God created for all mankind to be a part of. Because man has become so prideful of themselves about trying to dominate people and things in this world; some people have become cold-hearted to the people as well as; to the cares of the people who live in this world.

Just as Pharaoh's heart was hardened in the Egyptian days; God has allowed such destruction in this world to take place because of the arrogance and the ignorance of mankind steady rejecting him. And by mankind continuing to disobey God and to not acknowledge God; for who he is and to what God has done concerning the world; bad things will continue to happen until God returns for those who are righteous.

Natural disasters are mentioned all throughout the world and man has no control over it. God is the one who controls everything but the world seems to have forgotten about God and his greatness of making this and making that to where some people would even dare to say that God doesn't exist or that there is no God. People mock God every day and are steady rejecting God.

In this day and time, it is very hurtful to be rejected and to not be accepted by anyone. But, to be rejected and to not be accepted by mankind the way that Jesus was and still is being rejected as well as denied; is heartbreaking. We must not continue to reject God or others because, we need God in our lives as well as we need others.

People are committing suicide, killing and destroying others because of being rejected by others, because they are being ridiculed, bullied and they don't seem to fit in or belong because of their gender, size, nationality or social status. If this bothers us, how do we think that Jesus felt or feels about being rejected and excluded from the lives of people that he died on the cross for to save from their sins and that still won't accept him?

Jesus stands in the gap for us even when we displease him; and the wrath of God isn't thrust upon the nation in full causing destruction of the end to this world because, of the blood of Jesus Christ; that was shed on the cross that God sees as Jesus pleas for our mercy.

Prayer is the solution to the problems of the world today. But, prayer is no longer permitted in our schools. Now, school killings are running rampant and lives have been destroyed severely. In order for the violence to begin to cease; our society as a whole needs to acknowledge God and to accept God in their heart so that change can began to take place.

God wants us to humble ourselves before him and seek after him but, so many people are turning to other things for refuge other than him; and this makes things worse for themselves instead of asking God for his help in the matter.

Some people reject God; just as some parents reject and neglect their own children or like some animals reject and neglect their own young. The question why is mind boggling, so sad but, yet true. It is unbelievable on how this can be done but, it happens too often every day, somewhere; and our nation as a whole are suffering from the consequences of these choices that are being made.

We must take responsibilities for our own actions that we make and include God in our life to help us to make rightful decisions concerning our life; as well as to the lives of others. God is Alpha and Omega for he is the beginning and the end. We are nothing without God and that's a true and stated fact when one reads the word of God.

The bible mentioned of wailing women but, now in today's time; everybody needs to lift up their voices to the Lord and wail for the cleanup of this sinful nation.

There is no time to keep playing with God or to keep being in denial of our need for God. This world is doomed to destruction because of its rejection to God. Just as the sinful cities were destroyed in biblical times; this world is coming to the same fate because of sin and disobedience which still exist among this evil generation.

Now is not the time to continue to reject God because, the world can end at any time and if one does not have God on their side and a part of their life when God does return for his true believers of him; then one will be forever lost and separated from him through all eternity where their real sorrows will began with no end.

The tables will one day turn on those who are rejecting God now, here on this earth for the Day of Judgment is coming; and it will be a day of rejection for the ones that God never knew because, they denied knowing him and refused to accept him as their Lord and Savior.

Don't let this happen to you!

Accept God now! Trust and believe in God now! Follow God now! Repent of your sins now!

We must not be ashamed to call on God's holy name. We must deny ourselves of the things of this world to be with the Lord and to live with the Lord forever.

One must not continue to accept the lies from the devil and his clan. Therefore, one must reject Satan and his plans. Which work against God.

One must turn from the madness and sadness of the devil and walk in the goodness and the gladness of the Lord.

We are made in God's image but man have placed themselves to be above God. Lucifer choose to let his ego rise as well but he spiraled and was kicked out of heaven and fell; along with a third of the angels to hell for following after Satan.

This is a prime example of all that choose to follow Satan today; on how they too will miss out in getting in heaven if they continue to ride and side with Satan as they choose to reject God.

God will not force anyone to love him or to accept him. This is a freewill choice. Just as Jesus choose to die for us and to save us from the sins of the world by shedding his blood on the cross for us; how could anyone reject him for the love that was selfless shown for us?

Jesus took our place and he bore the pain and the shame while taking the blame of our sins upon himself.

In closing, those who choose to deny Christ will suffer the consequences from their own actions of following Satan. Jesus is the way, the truth and the light so, choose today where you wish to stay.

Those last two words were never spoken nor realized
Through the precious unspoken love as one lies
Though thinking back now; it was said in your eyes.

Another anticipated anniversary day now come and go
Only to sit and wonder why didn't I know; as the tears yet flow
From remainders of lovely cards and gifts of love that's left to show.

The days seem sad and gray since you've been away
And at the close of each day; I'm still left with hardly anything to say.

I'm lost and empty on the inside
Pained and drained from silent tears that I've cried
Trying desperately to memorize
All the beautiful things you've said to me
Before you took to the heavenly skies.

That fretful Thursday morning you never said to me
that this was our last day together, Sweetie.
But if our eyes could speak what was to be
Our last good – bye was spoken through thee.

While lying awake in bed all day
I thought and wondered what to pray
Not really knowing what I should say
Only hoping, just hoping that time passes away.

Missing you is painfully so
Oh how I wish you didn't have to go.
As confusion brings such woe
While the illusion gives yet a blow.

I battle through the conscience mind
From being yet left behind.
Plagued with memories of you and I that are oh, so real
As day after day time seems to stand still.

The thoughts of days gone by travel through my head
As I toss and I turn in my bed
Reaching for you; but only finding emptiness instead.

The slap of reality snaps me fully awake
Clarifying that this isn't fake
Yet realizing each passing day that it's not a mistake.

While I mope and I cope with the loss that I feel
Saying to myself that I wasn't given a raw deal
Knowing that he is in God's will
Yet.... at the end of the day; time seems to only stand still.

CHAPTER 4

"On Your Feet Soldier"

RECESS IS OVER

When I think about recess, I think about playtime of little children outside enjoying themselves, running, skipping, laughing and just simply cute, adorable little darlings having fun without a care in the world. This scene of course is beautiful and lovable but, all good things must come to an end because eventually, we must grow up and get down to business so, with that being said: Recess is over!

Some of us are no longer at the level of immaturity for we have become adults and we do things differently than we did when we were children; now, we are on the mature level and we have put away childish thinking and childish things.

We all were designed to move from different stages of life which helped us to develop into the man or the woman that God made us out to be. However, there comes a time in a person's life when one must become serious about things that concern them in this life.

Therefore, we all need to get serious about our relationship with God because God is real and he isn't a play toy and God doesn't want us to keep playing with him as if he is. Meanwhile, we should reference God for who he is and get more focused about things that pleases God the most; which includes our soul.

God's judgment is soon to come upon us and we should get real with God and be real about the things that are of God. God wants us to be serious about our commitment to him. This is no playing matter because the day of God's wrath is not going to be a laughing matter or a tap on the wrist.

Yes! God is a loving and a forgiving God but we can't continue to live for God one minute and then turn around and live for the devil the next minute and say; "God knows my heart."

Yes! We know that God knows every body's heart and he understands each of us perfectly but, apparently we don't understand ourselves since we continue to play theses silly little games with God.

Some of us need to put our own selves in time out so that we can have time to reflect on how good God has truly been to us and maybe we will realize that playtime truly is over and take heed to the things that we do that could be hurtful to ourselves.

There truly is a time for everything and there will come a time in life where we wish that we could start over again and do things a little bit differently and there won't be anything that we can do over to receive a different outcome.

But, if we take time out now from our hectic schedules and let God lead and guide us in our life; then everything will turn out right and we wouldn't wish to change a thing because God will be in total control of everything that we do or say and all will be alright.

I remember as a little girl, how my mother would make me sit on the floor at the corner of her bed because I was disruptive and fussing with my younger brother and twin sister; so, she would separate me from them by doing this as my punishment until my attitude became better.

I had time to think about a lot of things that I did wrong in that length of time of me sitting alone as I missed out on being with my siblings laughing and watching cartoons. My mother eventually let me go back to join in with them and I returned with a much better outlook than I started out with and my attitude was more grateful and more loving to everyone and I appreciated everything because I was a much better person afterwards.

I had time to myself to regroup and to reflect on things that I had done that landed me in the predicament that I was in and I tried hard not to do it again so that I wouldn't have to sit alone and miss out on playing with my two younger siblings again.

It is time out for us thinking that God is pleased with us coming to him only when we need something from him. God wants us to realize that we need him every day and not just when we are having a bad day and things are all out of whack and may have become slack.

There are times when things are truly over in our life and we need God's help to help us to pick up our feet and move into the direction where he wants us to be.

Just as when death comes along and we can't change the outcome of it; what has been done, has been done. It's very sad to say but, we must ask God to help us to accept it and by faith keep moving; otherwise, the pain and the grief will take us down.

After-all, God won't put more on us than we can bear because God will be right there to help us get through the heartache of it all; so that we won't fall.

As a true warrior for God, we must get back on our feet and get back in the saddle for the battle isn't over yet.

Living for God is not a playing matter for our mind has to be made up to be on this battle ground for the Lord. We must be sharp and on our feet ready to move whenever it's time to move, listening for any sound and not playing around.

The devil is always out to kill, steal and to destroy and he doesn't play fair because he simply doesn't care. Therefore, we have to keep our guards up by staying prayed up to be informed of his next move that we must execute on demand.

We will always be ahead of the devil when we listen and obey God's plans. But, how can one know God's plan?

First, one must know God and be a true believer of God so that one will follow God through the leading of God's Holy Spirit. Then once we are instructed by God; we must not drag our feet towards getting the task at hand done to take care of business in leading others to Christ.

There is a time limit for everything and only God knows when the time is up for all mankind here on earth. Meanwhile, we must not continue to ignore God by doing the things that we want to do.

God is trying to get our attention to help us to stay focused on the things that matters the most which is: our salvation and the salvation of others. Therefore, we have no time to lag and drag around. Our life and the lives of others are at stake while we continue to play. God is coming back whether we are ready or not and we must be making preparations by living a holy lifestyle when God does return for his people.

The angels of the Lord will be sent with a great sound of a trumpet and it will be heard from all around by all mankind and we must not be found without our work undone for God. Therefore, we must get our house in order and be prepared, ready and alert at all times by being watchful because no man knows the hour or the day that the Lord shall appear.

In closing, this world as we know it is coming to its end and only those who have placed their hope in Christ will be permitted to enter in to live forever in heaven with Jesus; our Lord and our friend.

As we all know, blood is very vital to our body for we need blood in our circulatory system to keep us functioning properly. In other words, we need blood to live. Blood represents life and blood flows throughout different parts of the organs in our body that helps us to circulate. Without blood flowing throughout our veins to various channels of the body; we will malfunction. Poor circulation of the blood destroys the ability to move the way we should which becomes weak and eventually deteriorates the mobility thereof. Just as we need blood; we all need Jesus who is the giver of life; and Jesus gave his life so that we could have life eternally.

Jesus shed his blood and died on the cross for all mankind so that we could live free from sin; therefore, we no longer have to be a slave to sin because, Jesus paid the penalty for our sin by being the ultimate sacrifice for all humanity through the shedding of his blood. Jesus' blood is rich and powerful and it cleanses us all from unrighteousness when we repent of our sins. DNA reveals what blood type we are and it tells who our father is. To be washed by the blood of Jesus represents that we are a child of God; which is to say an heir of God and joint heirs with Christ.

Only Jesus can wash away our sin once we receive him and let him come into our life for when Jesus died on the cross and rose from the grave with all power in his hands; now, Satan no longer has hold over anyone who wants to be free from sin. We are free to rise up out of situations that tried to hold us down and to keep us bound by walking in the newness of God's righteousness doing the will of God and not the likes of the Devil.

We can be made whole just like the woman with the issue of blood became free of her infirmity of 12 long years by stepping out on faith touching the helm of the Savior's garment. We can be delivered just like Naaman was cleansed of his leprosy by humbling himself and by being obedient to the instructions of Elisha; the prophet of God to wash himself 7 times in the Jordan River. Our life can be spared just like the Hebrew Children's lives were spared by them placing the lamb's blood on the door post of their house for death to pass over them.

Many people's lives today, have been spared through the help of blood donors who choose to give some of their blood to help in times of crisis; for others who may be in need of blood. I personally would like to thank God for allowing blood donors to give of themselves to help save others' lives because, I may not be here today had it not been for someone taking the time out to donate their blood so that I could receive it.

I had a total of not (1) but (2) blood transfusions within a 3 month span. It was very scary and very vital because I had 3 tumors removed from my stomach and I began to hemorrhage shortly after surgery from the removal of the tumors. A lot of blood was lost but, thank God that he allowed death to pass over me.

It feels good to know that I was and that I am covered under the blood of Jesus and that he pulled me through all of that to be alive today to say this: that I am still here and standing strong holding up the blood stained banner for Jesus.

Where would I be; had it not been for the Lord on my side?

There are many people today; who are alive as well through blood transfusions and even dialysis which helps to assist in saving people's lives. Thank God for the doctors and nurses as well as the machines for their special skills, services and training to administer to those who are in need of their help to continue their life. For these were ways of lives being saved through the blood.

Now, I will speak a little about how lives have been changed through the shedding of blood. The first murder was committed by Cain killing his brother Abel all because of jealousy.

There is so much jealousy in this world today where innocent lives are being destroyed over petty and silly things and it's damaging to us all. God gave us life and we should all value life; and not take life. Too much blood is being spilled and is thought of as a thrill to some and sends a chill to others. This must not continue to be for God is not pleased by life being taken by thee.

How can we continue to take the lives of our sisters/brothers; of our fathers/mothers of our children or simply the lives of any other? We all are family being part of God's grand creation standing together as one. We must not continue to hate or to discriminate against one another and have blood on our hands towards any man.

Jesus gave his life as ransom for our life. Therefore, we must remember that the blood that Jesus shed was to cleanse us and to bring us all together in the end. After-all, "Blood is thicker than water" and we must join together and stop the madness of killing; for we all are created equally. We all have sinned and come short of the glory of God and nothing but the blood of Jesus can wash away our sins.

We must not continue to be divided for we are "one nation under God" and there will be justice for all one day by God. We must never forget why Jesus came. And, we must never forget what Jesus did for us all.

Jesus' death wasn't easy and he chose willingly to endure the pain as well as the shame and took the blame for all of our names. "What manner of man is this" to do such a thing as this?

No one today, should live their life as if the blood that Jesus shed for us was no big deal or as if it didn't matter because, it most definitely was important and it most certainly did matter and he didn't have to do it; but he did. Because he loves us so much he made that ultimate decision that only he could do; for the will of his father to redeem man from the snares of the enemy.

We must not let the blood that Jesus shed for us be in vain by continuing to live life insane doing any and everything that's affiliated with Satan.

Before Jesus' death on the cross; people under the old covenant could only approach God through a priest or with an animal sacrifice to be forgiven of their sins. Now, by the blood of Jesus and his death all people may go to God for themselves in faith for forgiveness of their sin because this is the seal of the new covenant.

Therefore, we must believe that Jesus died and rose for us and we must believe by faith that we are saved through grace. We no longer have to deny Christ for he is our mediator and he is at the right hand of the father interceding on our behalf; our petition to having eternal life is only through Jesus Christ; our Savior, Lord and King.

One day we will come to realize and to recognize who Jesus really is. Because, Jesus is the Messiah and he paid for the remission of sin through the shedding of his precious blood and we all have been counted worthy of forgiveness through his selfless sacrifice of himself; in our place.

We are justified by his blood and are spared from the wrath of God through Jesus Christ and through God's grace and his mercy; we are saved.

Therefore, we must never forget about the great sacrifice that Jesus endured for us in order for us to have salvation. We must be found without a spot or a wrinkle concerning our lifestyle when God returns for his true believers.

We must be pure and white as snow; being worthy to be among the Lamb of God and the 144,000 who endured the trials and the temptations of this world to be able to receive the many rewards as well as the crown of life for being faithful and committed to Christ until the very end.

In closing, during our walk with the Savior; we are never alone. If we should get tired or may feel too overwhelmed to continue on; we must look to the Cross of Calvary; where Jesus is sitting on the throne.

Going on in this life sometimes isn't easy but; when we're holding on to God's strength instead of trying to go forth alone in our own strength then we won't fall. We must hold our head up and just stand knowing that God will see us through. Even in the mist of our troubles or sorrows; we must stand boldly for the Lord and know that God will fight our every battle. People may talk about us or perhaps they may even try to do harm to us but, we can't run and hide like the disciples did when Jesus was being crucified – No!! We must stand tall on the Lord's side through the pressure and through the pain while calling on God's holy name, believing that God will bring about a change.

Sometimes, we may even feel weak or often feel all alone but Jesus is the one to call on for he will give us the power to be strong. We must give our all and push our way through no matter how tired and frustrated to what we may feel. God will help us because God's not dead; he's alive and real. We must take advantage of our situation knowing that whenever we take a stand for righteousness that we will prevail. Therefore, we should not let anyone dissuade us from doing what's right no matter who they are.

God is on his way back for his true believers and we have work to do until he comes. Standing on the word of God and holding on to our faith in God is what we must rely on to get us through our dark stages and phases of this life's journey. True believers in Hebrews Chapter 11; held on to their faith and trust in God being tested and tried and have made it over safely to the other side.

We too, must continue to stand boldly for the Lord; showing others that we, now live to tell the world about God who never fails.

Not only do we have the power to walk right or the power to talk right but, we also have the power to live right because the power of the living God compels us to do what's right. Having the power of God all the way around; which lives on the inside of us. There is no need to be afraid to stand for God because; "Greater is he that lives in you than he that is in the world."

I am forever reminded about how afraid the disciples were when Jesus was crucified and how they ran to hide because they were terrified! But, Oh! How happy they were when they realized that Jesus was alive. They then; stood boldly to proclaim the name of Jesus when the spirit fell upon them and commissioned them to tell the world.

We too, can now proclaim to the world for all to experience this miraculous transformation for themselves once they will stand up for Christ.

We must not be ashamed to call on God's name. One does not have to continue to deny Christ. Jesus rose from the grave and we no longer have to be a slave to sin. We must stand up for what is right and fight for our life in this world which is filled with hatred against God's people. Meanwhile, we must not be afraid to stand for righteousness.

Queen Esther stood up for her people as well as for herself in Esther Chapter 4 by going to see the king uninvited. Haman had a death decree against all of the Jews in Persian Europe because he had hatred and bitterness for Mordecai; who did not and who would not bow down to him. Therefore, Haman intended to exonerate Mordecai and all of his people.

There comes a time in every man's life when they are faced with the ultimate challenge of the testing of their faith in God. There may even be times in our life where we will have to stand alone. Our friends or family members may not always agree to our decisions or our faith walk in Jesus Christ but, we must always do what we know is right by standing firm in our walk and God will give us strength to continue on.

No matter how painful and unbearable things may seem to us; we must keep standing on the word of God in spite of how things may look; we will make it through the test and the trials if we faint not. When one says; "For God I will live and for God I will die" then one is saying that they will go through whatever it takes regardless of how hard the task maybe to stay with the Lord.

Men and women of God have been martyred during their test and trials over the ages of life and they have been a true and firm believer for Christ. The devil is on his job 24/7 and we must be on our job being a real warrior for God by resisting him. Nothing is worth us compromising our salvation for. The trick of the enemy is out to destroy us. Therefore, we can't give in to moments of pleasure or beautiful treasures. Like Esau giving his birthright to his brother Jacob for a bowl of pottage because he was hungry.

God gives us power to keep our feet treading through the thick and dark valleys that we stagger through. Therefore, we don't have time to grumble or mumble about anything. Meanwhile, we must stand; even when we are under pressure and our backs may seem to be up against the wall. We must stand on the solid rock of Jesus Christ and know that he will deliver us if we call.

In closing, we must hold on tight for dear life to the Savior's hand, never letting go and take a bold stand. No one knows when God will return but we must know who we are in Christ and stand firm. One day all of our troubles will be over but until that day of the Lord comes, we must stand on guard and take cover.

Back in biblical times in the Old Testament scriptures; war between the Northern Kingdom and the Southern Kingdom were fought over and over. Today, the nations are feuding still over this and over that with many lives yet being destroyed.

We battle in our minds; wondering if things will ever change for the better and only those who have hope in Christ can surely rest assure because, payday is coming for all who believe on our Lord and Savior; Jesus Christ.

Many things that we face in this life are just a testing of our faith and we must be willing and able to go through the challenges just like we would an obstacle course to reach the other side of it.

There have been generations before us who have gone on striving through many severe and unforeseen challenges while, struggling to reach their goal and only through their faith and their perseverance; they were able to make it over.

We, too, must proceed in this life no matter what is tossed out at us to discourage us from receiving our just reward at the end of this life's journey.

God has great things in store at the end of the road for us. But, how are we going to receive it if we never make up our mind to follow God and take the steps necessary that will lead us down the path to him?

Payday is coming after while and only those that have been walking by faith in God and who have stayed in the race for God; will receive that pay.

Jesus went to prepare a place for us and we can only imagine how it's going to look surrounded by the things that God has in store for those who truly love him because, no one knows nor has anyone seen this place yet. But, we can rest assure that it will be amazing.

There is more up ahead that God has for us if we hang on to him until he returns again for us and we should not miss out in receiving it because we gave up or turned from him too soon.

Just as we receive pay from our job, or just as we may receive paid vacation from having a job for time invested on the job; we will receive a heavenly reward after our faithful earthly mission of working for God and trusting as well as believing in God is complete. Therefore, we must put forth time and effort to God; to receive our eternal reward from God.

We don't have time to doubt while in route; for "we walk by faith and not by sight" enduring the fight for our life.

Meanwhile, we must look to Jesus; "the author and finisher of our faith"; the only one who can truly help us and the only one who truly cares about us in our time of need. Because, he is the hope to our soul towards us having a better life once this world is over.

Therefore, we must push forward day by day in the strength that God will constantly give us and focus on the incorruptible reward that God has for us. Besides, we shouldn't dwell on negative things that are happening around us that could cause us to lose sight of our plight towards making it into heaven. In the meantime, we must take the initial stand to do all that we can to make it into that brand new land; that Jesus went away to prepare for us.

There is plenty of work yet to be done because souls have yet to be witnessed to concerning them giving their life to Christ. We have no time to sit back and relax on God; while so many people are in need of God. Therefore, we must get out and go forth in telling others about the Savior of the world who can, and who will deliver them from their sin; if they will only repent and receive him to come into their life.

God's commission for all mankind is not hard to endure; because, it is easy when one has their mind made up to live for God and when one is committed to do the will of God. Telling others about God and his goodness is carefree and we should be willing as well as able to share the good news to all about Jesus Christ to help lost souls find peace and rest in Jesus Christ; of whom their soul seeks for in this life.

Yes! Payday for all believers in Christ is just over the horizon to God's new kingdom that is prepared for his followers. And everyone has an opportunity to receive a righteous payment from God by being in the will of God; while being a true witness for God.

We are living in the last days and those who pretend to be a follower of Christ will be weeded out by falling under to Satan's tricks. Those who are actually true to God will with stand the lies and the deceits of the evil forces and therefore, will not give in and be against God.

The devil's reign over this world is coming to its bitter end and he is out to recruit as many as he can to be on his side against God. And only, the true believers in Christ will be able to resist and defeat the devil's power through the help of God's Holy Spirit that reveals the truth and shines the light on such wickedness of the vicious attempts that are being displayed to try to pull them away; from God.

No matter what may come our way to try to hinder us from going forth in this life; we must stand firm in our faith to God and continue to be a real soldier for God; knowing that we have help in God to defend us in times of trouble. God is our refuge and just as God is preparing for the final battle over the enemy in Revelations Chapter 19; we can't afford to miss out on this great victory that will take place towards the destruction of Satan. Meanwhile, we must stay busy doing the work of the Lord so that we won't get side tracked and turn back from the Lord.

In closing, God's judgment day is on the way and every man will receive his just pay. Valuable time spent with God now is on the line; for God could return at any time.

Many people in this world today give a lot of time towards doing for others or themselves but seem to have hardly any time at all to give for God. True, God wants us to do for others; especially the disabled, the needy, the elderly, the homeless, the lost, the widows, the children and etc. But, we can't forget about God; the creator while we go about doing for others.

We must clear our calendars and take time out from our so-called busy schedules and spend quiet and alone time with God. Just as Jesus went and prayed to his Father in Luke Chapter 5; we, too, must do the same by talking to God in prayer.

Like Jesus took time from being among the great multitude of people; we often become weak from doing so many other tasks and fail to realize that we need strength to continue. God is our source of strength that we need daily to continue to do anything at all in this life and when we cut the source off; then we are running solo on our own which will eventually give out.

We simply, are nothing without God no matter how much we think that we are and have accomplished in our lives; take the time just to stop and think for a moment....

Who gave us the ability to do the things that we do or to have the things that we have?

Again, I will stress that we are nothing without God and we would have nothing had it not been for the grace of God's love and his mercy that he gives to us daily.

So, just as we walk and talk with people of this world every day throughout the day; God longs for us to walk and to talk with him. Just as we thank and praise others; God longs for us to thank and to praise him for his goodness. Just as we show and give love to others; God wants it from us too; for he deserves it and he should be #1 at the very top of all of our list daily; of whom we should acknowledge.

We should spend precious time with God every day; because of who God is and because of what God has done and is yet doing for us daily; all day. God requires so little of us in return and this is how the world repays him by ignoring him? Or this is how the world repays him by forgetting about him?

Yes, indeed! How little of us?

How can we not want to spend time in God's presence or how can we leave God out of our life while living in such an evil day and time as this? We must make the time and we must take the time to spend time with God for ourselves. We can't ride along on others coat tails to get what we always need from God through other people's prayers. Therefore, we must get in personal contact; one-on-one with God for ourselves.

Just like some guys go one-on-one in a basketball game or toe-to-toe in a game match; we, too, have to go head up with God and we must man up or woman up and take responsibility for our own actions concerning our salvation that we can only have through our Lord and Savior; Jesus Christ.

God loves us so much that he gave his only begotten son, Jesus; to die on the cross for our sins and it's because of the sacrifice of Jesus' blood; that we are made free once we believe in him and accept him in our heart. Therefore, we should take the first step heading in God's direction by opening the door of our heart and accept Jesus to come into our life because he is waiting patiently on us to let him in and to be a part of us.

God speaks to each of us daily and we must not continue to keep ignoring him or keep shutting him out of our life. He wants to help us but' we must want his help by answering to his call.

No matter how it may look or no matter how it may seem or feel to us; like we have everything in control or going on as some would say; we really and truly don't have things "made in the shade" when we don't have God in the equation of our life.

Meanwhile, we can't continue to leave God out of our life because, no man knows when their time is up; here in this lifetime. We also can't keep running from God nor, can we keep pretending to ourselves that we can make it without God being in our life.

I am a living witness that things will never be totally right in anyone's life without God being the center of their life; because, once people wake up and realize how truly wonderful and amazing that God is; they will let nothing or no one come between them spending time being in the presence of God. For there is no other experience that can measure up with how one feels to be surrounded by so much love.

No man's love or no man's touch can compare to what God has to share or to add to our life. One touch of God's love feels like a warm spot in the sun that one longs for on a cloudy, cold day. Or, perhaps; a warm blanket that's placed over you as you lay shivering from the chill of the cold. God's love fills you up on the inside; like drinking a nice, warm cup of coffee in front of a toasty fireplace where you wish to stay all day.

Spending time with God; makes you think of a happy couple being freshly in love; where one can hardly wait to be with the other and their conversation seems to last for hours and hours throughout the day with long, cuddled walks on the beach or the communication on the phone seems to never cease. For one is happy all over and it feels remarkable.

This is my example of what time spent with God feels like to me and his love is forever real and oh, what a thrill!!

Yes! Spending time with God is truly refreshing and uplifting! You feel light as a feather, as you cast all of your cares upon him and let God take complete control of any and every situation that you alone couldn't handle. It's truly incredible!

Who wouldn't want to feel like this every day; from a loving God who truly cares about them; while spending time being in the presence of him?

This is only 1 of the many simple things that is denied to God by so many people in this world; and that's spending time with him. God wants to have love returned to him as well and as much as God loves us he wants us to love him back.

God wants us to love him through us spending time with him in prayer daily and through our acceptance of him. Just as we want others to love and accept us; God wants it too.

Why is it so hard for people to love God? And why wouldn't people want to spend time with such a loving and caring God?

These two questions asked is truly beyond my thinking!!

Just as it's heartbreaking to see a child or a pet neglected or abused; it too is heartbreaking to God; for his creation of us to keep neglecting him. Every day, all day very heartbreaking indeed!!

Some people joy ride with friends all day; just about every day; and some people seem to party all night passing the time away and continuously leave God out of their lives without a care. God is fed up on how the world misuses and abuses him! Yet God, still loves us and gives us his grace and his mercy every day.

We must not continue to live our life carelessly. God wants us to get closer to him so that he will get closer to us keeping us safe and secure in his arms; away from the enemy's charm. But, God is not going to force us to spend quality time with him so the decision is fully our choice on whether we want to or not. But, in order to bring about a positive change into our life; we must make time for God in our life.

We must be like Mary; and take time out to sit at the feet of Jesus; having more love for him and being more concerned about what his purpose is and what his plans are to actually be a blessing towards others. We may not have expensive oil to pour on the feet of Jesus but, we can cry out to God with our tears and yes, he will see and hear us. God knows our heart and he feels our pain whenever we call on his holy name. Meanwhile, we must not be ashamed to take time out to spend with Jesus.

Therefore, we must give our devotion to God first and foremost than anything that exist in our life. God is a jealous God and we aren't to have or to place anyone or anything before him. We also shouldn't let other things come between us serving God either. Which includes one holding church titles and doing church duties as well; because holding church titles or participating in church positions does not guarantee our salvation so one must be very careful and not become comfortable and become slack by being deceived by the enemy from doing man's will of them and not the will of God.

We are saved by the grace of God; having a personal relationship with God; which is of more importance to God than one being too busy with church functions that one omits or fails to hear the word of God being preached or perhaps; of one neglecting to make time to be in prayer with God.

Despite however our busy schedule may become; we must make ourselves available to spend time with God and his ministry and use our God given abilities to the honor and glory of God and not man. Therefore, making time to be in God's presence daily is very crucial to a Saint of God. We must spend time talking to God in prayer to be made aware of the traps and the snares that the devil tries to set up to catch us off guard with.

In closing, we have not entered into the kingdom of God yet; so, we must continue to seek God daily for our guidance by making time and spending time in the presence of God throughout our walk with God.

We are living in the last days and the world is in so much uproar over this and over that. Many people are wondering about their future here on this earth and they don't know who they can turn to for help. Some people are making investments in many different companies trying to come up with a plan; putting their hopes and dreams into many things as they rely on man.

It's just about that time again for the voting season to begin and there are candidates on the ballet who promise to do this and who promise to do that; towards making things better for the people living in society hoping to gain their vote.

Some of these candidates even portray to have great credentials and pride themselves of being qualified by holding many titles for a vast number of years. Some even wear a wide smile on their face that often hides their disguise with a twinkle in the eyes; that often cover up their lies. Like a wolf in sheep's clothing trying to hide who they really are on the inside.

Some people in this world have a rather flawless image of themselves and they may look as if they are the best person to carry out the job that is designed to help make a difference in this life but; only God knows their real motives to what they are out to do and only God knows what they are truly capable of.

A lot of people in our society today, make many promises that they won't keep. They will try to gain our trust by lying to us; which deceives us; for they will say one thing and do just the opposite of what they said; never intending to do the right thing from the get go.

Man will simply lie to us having no remorse or regret for the pain that he may cause us and man will fail us but, God cannot lie and God will never fail us because he truly loves us and he looks out for us.

God hates a liar and God has a designated, fire burning place in store just for those who continue to lie deliberately to others; trying to get by in this world.

We, as a people must be very careful of whom we select to represent us in this day and time because, everyone who portray to be true are not always looking out for us or our best interest in this life and they may be out to only make life better for themselves as well as to the people with whom they affiliate with.

Therefore, we must look to God for his guidance concerning every decision that we choose to make in this life that's guaranteed to help us along this life's journey. Also, each of us have the power to make a difference in our own lives by casting our personal vote for Jesus. This decision is vitally important because, being a follower of Jesus Christ; will truly change your life. And having Jesus as the head of your life; will help you to make better decisions in this life.

We must cast our vote for Jesus today and we must not continue to delay. The normal way to cast a vote today in our Judicial System is done in secret; in a booth known as: a secret ballet like the old way of one confessing one's sins in secret at a confession booth with a priest. But, today, when one should cast their vote for Jesus; one doesn't have to cast for him in secret nor, does one have to wait for a special time of day, night or year; for we can run to Jesus at any time or we can give our life to Jesus by calling on him without fear and he will hear.

Jesus died on the cross for our sins publicly and he bore our sin and shame in pain; so, we must stand on our own two feet to cast our vote for Jesus and proclaim our victory of defeat from the enemy; in Jesus' name with no shame.

There is no excuse to continue to live in fear because Jesus; our Lord and Savior rose from the grave with all power being yet near; and this is no lie my dear. All of the world must open their ears to hear this good news about Jesus; so that they too, will shout and cheer!

There's a song in my heart from days of ole that says: "Nothing is impossible if you trust in God. Nothing is impossible if you believe upon his word. There is no secret to what God can do cause what he does for others he will do the same for you. Nothing is impossible if you trust in God."

Therefore, we must vote for Jesus every day because, Jesus is on our side and he is in our corner every step of the way. For Jesus died brutally and he shed his blood for us now, no other man has done that; nor, can any credentials top that!

Yes! Imagine that and believe that!

Jesus, the son of the living God; came down from his heavenly throne to save us from sin; to one day relieve us from all of the turmoil of this world that we all now live in. Jesus is the only one who can save us because, Jesus is the Savior of the world. Jesus is the way, the truth and the life. Jesus is the Rose of Sharon. Jesus is the lily of the valley and the bright and morning star. Jesus is a way maker, a strong tower, a doctor, a lawyer, a comforter, a friend, a mother and a father, a sister and a brother, a provider, a deliverer, a keeper, a healer, a fortress, a rock, a shield and buckler, a redeemer for Jesus is our all-in-all and he will never let us fall.

Now, these are only just a few of Jesus' guaranteed, flawless credibility or good deeds that we can rely on when we believe on Jesus. Jesus is the

Alpha and the Omega; he's the beginning and the end. We must put our faith and trust in him to certainly win. He's our hope for tomorrow; relieving all of our sorrow.

Whenever we may feel lost and all alone; I recommend Jesus for he's the one to call on. He will pick you up and he will turn you around as he places your feet on solid ground. So, rest assure Jesus will never let you down.

We can call on Jesus anytime. So, cast your vote for Jesus; our one, and only true friend.

In closing, Jesus is the only hope in this world today; for he's the light that leads the way. Only lift up your head and see; how to walk through such misery. Holding tight to the Savior's hand; who has definitely set you free.

Thoughts of you linger and mingle in my mind
Which are forever frozen of moments in time.

No more warmth of your strong hands to hold
Which leaves me feeling empty and cold.

Disconnected from your gentle and loving embrace
Longing to see that beautiful smile that once lit your face.

Oh, how I miss your sweet magnetic kiss
Which by the way, gave me such bliss.

The sound of your deep, mesmerizing voice; that once called my name
Leaves me only thinking that I hear you;
but it is definitely not the same.

Then reality steps in; as my thoughts of you slowly drift away
For I'd rather have you here with me instead;
on this Anniversary Day!

Retracting the days in my mind
Trying desperately to find
How my world became so unkind
As your time slowly unwind.

Before my eyes your life did travel
As life between us began to unravel
Gave my mind such a scrabble
And only words left to babble.

While precious moments together flew
Feeling Oh so alone, so sad and so blue
Without a clue of what to do.

I still count down the day
From which you went away.
Today makes 365 days which is a year
And there hasn't been a day without a tear.

Life without you is definitely not the same
And I must admit I still mention your name
For I love you and I miss you still
And I know that I always will.

CHAPTER 5

"Onward Christian Soldier"

THE POWER OF THE TONGUE

*E*very day people somewhere are talking about something whether it's on the radio, in the news, in a check-out line, on the screen or on the scene; words are spoken from the powerful device of the tongue. Some words that we say are relatively important while, other things that are said may be rather negative and could be kept to ourselves.

The words that we say should be seasoned with grace; showing compassion and concern while being mindful as well as respectful to others. We can get our message out or our point across to others through kind words spoken rather than through harsh words that often leave someone feeling broken.

The words that we choose to speak can also get us into a lot of trouble; therefore, we should choose our words of what we say wisely. God's Holy Spirit will give us the self-control that we need to help us to admonish the things that we should say to one another. However, what's on the inside of our heart will reveal itself on the outside of us. In other words, what's in you, will come out of you whether it's good or whether it's bad. A lot of times; things come to surface once the pressure is turned up in our life and the actions and words unfold.

The bible says in James 3:8; "But the tongue can no man tame; it is an unruly evil, full of deadly poison." Only God can help us to change; for he is the one who will give us the will power to have self-restraint over our actions or our sayings once we repent of our sins and accept him to come into our life to clean us up from within.

When conflicts arise, we should be eager to hear what is being discussed and not be so hasty to address the issue and think things through before placing judgment. It is so easy to lash out when we are angry but, we must try to control ourselves and not jump the gun by saying things that can't always be taken back once it has been said.

We should take time out to listen carefully before we voice our opinion about this, that or the other because; listening attentively to the matter can result in a more gentle response than for one to reply with loud and rude outbursts through anger of the situation on hand towards taking things out of context and feelings or perhaps, lives become destroyed.

For just as our words can help to bless someone; our words can also hurt and curse someone. Some people use slander, some use degrading and belittling words that could hurt our pride and often destroys others which sometimes causes them to commit suicide. We must not be a stumbling block to anyone with our words, deeds or our actions. We must be led by God's spirit with what to say, when to say and how to say with what needs to be said that will be beneficial to all who are in need of a word from God.

Proverbs 18:21 says; "Death and life are in the power of the tongue: and they that love it shall eat the fruit thereof.

We have the power to speak life into our situations towards our everyday lives and we also have the power to speak destruction to come upon ourselves as well when we speak negatively into the atmosphere of our circumstances.

I am a living testimony and I am alive today; because, I spoke life to myself that beautiful, sunny, Saturday morning. My three young sons at the time and myself were going to enjoy ourselves together at the park but, first I needed to wash my car. I drove inside of this automatic car wash facility, put the required amount of money in the machine, followed the instructions to proceed through and stopped for the car wash cycle to begin. The water began to spray out and to run down the windows. Then the soap started to mix in and to foam; covering the windows from all sides and then the front windshield. During this washing process; I heard a still small voice that was so calm and so clear that I still hear over and over in my mind today; that I've never heard before that particular day say: "Turn your windshield wipers on" by the way, I have never in my life done this before but I didn't hesitate to turn my wipers on as I was instructed to do and I did just that..... I turned on my windshield wipers and there before us were 3 young men blocking the entrance of the car wash and I knew without a shadow of a doubt through God's discerning spirit within me that mischief was on their mind and I felt that they were going to rob me and possibly kill me. It's as if we read each other's mind when our eyes met once those wipers washed away those suds from my blinding windshield. A smirk came across one of the young men's face who was sitting in the back seat of that vehicle as we continued to stare at one another. They slowly drove away as we continue to watch each other and when they were out of sight, tears fell from my eyes as I began to tremble and I couldn't get out of that car wash fast enough as I kept repeating desperately: Lord, I want to live Lord, I want to live and God granted me life for I remember days earlier as I would look in the obituary section of the newspaper and see people I knew; I'd ask God why not me instead of them because; I am the one who don't want to be here. But, that particular Saturday morning I woke up and I spoke life by calling on the phone to people and saying to them that I wanted to live not knowing why I felt like living and God gave me that chance to live that day in the car wash that I see clearly in my mind right now over and over again freshly as a reminder that life and death really is in the power of the tongue. I still wipe away tears as I speak about it to this day because the incident is seared in my memory just as if it happened yesterday and I can't help but to say; thank you Lord for sparing my life!

Therefore, we must be extra careful about what we say because, our tongue is a powerful weapon and our words that we say can burn like fire; or our words that we speak can help to save us in harmful situations.

Meanwhile, we should be quick to listen to those that have a controlled and caring tongue because they give wise and truthful advice; for their words will help to encourage us and not seek to destroy us. While on the other hand, there are those that have a careless and conniving tongue that we should avoid listening to because these are those who will say just about anything through lies, curses and gossip which causes the anger and the destruction of others.

In closing, God spoke the world into existence and we as his children have the power to speak healing and blessings into our own lives and into the lives of others as well.

With many of the things that are programmed through our mind from the things that we may see on the news, from all of the chaos and the calamity around the world; I am so glad to know that God will keep us in perfect peace whose mind is stayed on him.

Therefore, we shouldn't allow our mind to be deceived by the cloudiness of negative things that we may often hear or that we may see. We have control over what we choose to perceive or receive in our mind by focusing our attention on things that we know to be lovely, holy, righteous, true and pure. Meanwhile, we must not be enticed by fantasy, evil, false or fiction things that can corrupt our thoughts.

I've often heard of this quote "A mind is a terrible thing to waste" and as a child; I didn't really realize what it meant but, as I got older; I thought about some foolish things that I've done down through the ages and stages of my life and recognized that the saying was true.

We must put our mind to good use and we can't let the devil have our thoughts by sitting down thoughtless. The saying; "an idle mind is the devil's workshop" allows Satan a chance to enter into our mind to try to control our thoughts to turn our thoughts into doing his thoughts.

Sometimes, we aren't fully aware of things that we do until it's gotten us into a heap of trouble and we need help getting out of jams that we often put ourselves into because, of mindless things that we do without thinking properly before we do them.

We must not let the world feed or corrupt our mind with filthy thoughts that can filter down into our heart and spirit and destroy us from the inside out. Therefore, we must feed our mind with more of the word of God to renew our mind, with the love of God that deters the negativity that wants to creep and to seep into our mind to unravel us.

Just as we must protect our heart; we must also protect our mind from allowing the trick of the enemy to disperse gossip or to distribute bad thoughts to enter into the mind. Meanwhile, we must not continue to be brain washed by the deceitful words that are not being truthfully told about God's holiness.

Therefore, we must put the word of God to use in our life to not be entertained by the deceiving words of false prophets who are leading so many astray from the true doctrine of God's truthful and holy word. We must study the word of God allowing God's word to speak to our mind and our heart as we meditate on his word daily which will then give us the ability to see and to know for ourselves; what the word of God truly says through the leading of God's spirit that's being revealed through his living word.

All believers have the mind of Christ; doing that which is pleasing to God and not the devil. We as true believers of God must do the will of God properly by having our mind equipped with the true word of God. For God's word is "a lamp unto our feet and a light unto our path" and it will lead and guide us into all truth.

Therefore, we must be able to think clearly about the things that come to our mind by being sober in our thinking; looking to Christ for hope, grace and mercy. We don't have time to waste by being confused over this and over that which may be fumbling and tumbling around in our head. Therefore, we must get a grip on things in this life that causes us to slip by having self-control towards staying focused on God until he comes.

So many people today in this world are letting drugs, gambling and alcohol take over their mind; thinking that they can quit anytime that they want to or thinking that AA or that rehabilitation is the ultimate cure of what is going on in their lives. Yes! Thank God for the help that some are receiving but, the actual cure to the problem on hand is for one to give one's life to God who is the winning plan.

One must take back the power from the devil by being mindful of how God loves us and how much God wants us to live by his standards and not of ourselves. For after-all, everything that God does is good and he wishes for us to prosper and be in good health while we are here on this earth.

Meanwhile, we must refresh our mind thinking more clearly and more positively about our life because, thinking rationally and logically could save our life.

We only hurt ourselves when we continue to do the things that Satan wants us to do which helps to destroy us. Satan does not look out for our best interest but, God does and if we allow the devil to keep instructing us to make bad decisions in life; then our life will continue to stay corrupt with harmful actions to ourselves.

We live in a world that is surrounded by sin and sin affects our mind as well as our heart with hatefulness and evilness of this world that wants to plague us with discriminative and destructive actions of our thoughts that are held within.

Only having a mind like Christ will one be able to resist the evil forces of this world and having a prayerful relationship with God will keep us motivated and stimulated towards doing the will of God.

In the meantime, we must not continue to overload our brain by trying to please man but rather, we should focus more and change our thought pattern towards trying to please God and to do the things in this life that will help to benefit us and that will not seek to destroy us.

We should thank God every day, throughout the day for keeping our mind. Because, so many people are battling with so many different things neurotically, mentally, emotionally in the mind such as: Dementia, Alzheimer, epilepsy, schizophrenia, depression, bipolar, anxiety, suicidal thoughts and the list goes on and on.

Medication stabilizes but God specializes and makes us new all over. Therefore, we don't have to worry when we turn the problem over to him. God is a mind regulator and everything will turn out fine when we keep our mind focused on him.

In closing, we must renew our mind daily in the word of God and allow God to transform us over in our thinking and in everything that we do or say which will please God in every way.

Many times in our lives we may have witnessed faith in action. Just as some people in biblical times saw firsthand the move of God in a life changing instant because of having faith in God. There are several incidents in the bible that took place and faith was a major role in it becoming into reality.

Like for instance: Peter walked on water, a blind man healed, the woman with the issue of blood made whole, Naaman dipped in dirty Jordan River 7 times to be cleansed of his leprosy, boy healed from seizures, Jesus feeds five thousand, the walls of Jericho came tumbling down, Mary Magdalene healed from 7 spirits, the 3 Hebrew boys delivered from the fiery furnace, the lame man walking, Daniel in the lion's den, Lazarus raised from the dead, Rahab hides the spies, legions of demons cast out of a man, Jonah in the belly of a whale, children of Israel walking on dry ground of The Departed Red Sea, Tabitha brought back to life and Ruth gleans in the field of Boaz. All of these people's lives were miraculously changed due to their action by their faith.

God wants us to live by faith in our walk with him; just like so many of God's people in the earlier generations did and received favor in the sight of God. We are the key towards helping others to live their life by faith through our testimonies of what God has done for us in our lives.

This is my personal testimony:

I was once involved in an adulteress relationship for 10 long miserable years and I was frozen in turmoil that wouldn't loosen its grip on me. I didn't know how to walk away or how to let go. I didn't know if I was coming or going. I didn't know if I should go backwards or forwards. But, I did know that I was tired of spinning my wheels and getting nowhere. Yes, I was tired of hitting a brick wall in my life and being made and played for a fool. I refused to stay any longer to where I was; because each day I was dying on the inside.

My spirit, my self-esteem, my dignity and my pride was torn and raging on the inside where I could no longer hide who I was and how I felt from the outside. I couldn't take it anymore the person I had become through the sin that had taken control over me and had invaded me as well as corrupted me.

So I cried out to the Lord in desperation like Peter cried out to Jesus to save him as he began to sink and like God reached out to help Peter; God reached out to help me to walk out of that hypnotizing, traumatizing and dramatizing situation through my faith and my belief in knowing who I truly belong to and to who I really am.

Then, the grip of sin fell from me with each step that I began to take in God's direction and right now, today, I am a free woman indeed, living my life by the grace of God through the power of faith. God rescued me from a life of bondage to sin and shame. So, what God did for me; he can and will do the same for others who are entangled with sin.

Therefore, we can be delivered from the trap of sin. God does not want us to rely on tarot cards, lottery tickets, palm readers, slot machines, high rolling, bank accounts, jobs, sugar daddies, sugar mommas or good-Luck to make ends meet in this word. God simply wants us to live by faith through relying totally on him to supply all of our needs in this life; according to his riches and glory in Christ Jesus. Most of the times; people will only call on God during their desperate moments; but what one fails to realize is that God is there always for us; during the good times as well as the bad times.

Faith without action is dead; therefore, we must put our faith into practice with God every day which will give us the assurance that God will help take care of the situations needed in our lives as he sees fit towards doing so. All one has to do is to walk away and keep looking ahead to God just as Peter walked on water while staying focused on God as well and God will save us should we begin to fail.

Having faith moves our loving God into providing miraculous actions of his divine handiwork that only he can address to the problem on hand.

When we truly learn how to live by faith of trusting and depending on God; we will be able to attest to the impossible taking place through the power of our faith; by our God.

Therefore, we must keep the faith for we all have a measure of faith that we should utilize when we are tempted and tried by Satan.

Job is a prime example of how we should live our life in God. Because, tragedies and heartbreaks come upon us to shake our faith and it test us to keep firm in our faith and our belief in God no matter what may come to try to destroy us or to cripple our walk with God.

Satan comes to "kill, steal and to destroy what God has blessed us with. But, what God has for us is for us; so, we must persevere through the storms of this life by our faith, hope, trust and dependency on God; knowing that troubles in our way won't last always.

Meanwhile, we must go through the fire holding on to God's hand; knowing also, that God has a plan for our life even if we can't always see what is around the corner; or what is approaching us up ahead. God knows the thoughts and the plans that he has for us which are of peace and goodwill up until the end.

You see, God clearly knows all and he sees all! We must walk through the variables of this life knowing that God is going to be with us until the very end of whatever it is that we will encounter.

However, our faith in God will hold the key towards the outcome of our situation, and we must fulfill the task because we are not alone; for the God of comfort is there to help us to be strong.

Therefore, we must cling on to our faith knowing that God will restore unto us everything that we may have lost if we don't receive it here on this earth; then God will take care of us in the afterlife in heaven.

We must stand even when it feels that we can't get up or even if we don't know why God may have allowed things to go array in our life. Things will turn out right and God will give us "double for our troubles" if we hold on to our faith in him.

Wallowing in self-pity gets us nowhere and it only shows the lack of faith that we may have in God. Therefore, we must turn to God in our weakness and in meekness knowing that he will deliver us from all of the confusion and the illusion that wants to bring us despair while being in his care. Meanwhile, God will continue to stand by us and give us the faith and the power to move along.

Rahab, (the harlot) made an ultimate decision and she hid the Israelite spies by faith and ended up saving herself and her whole household from the destruction of death. We may not always know what to do but when we learn to trust God and move by faith; positive results will take place; showing us that God is there and in control of everything.

Furthermore, no one knows what tomorrow holds; we must continue to live our life and let things unfold by the hands of God as we touch him with our faith.

The bible tell us that; "The just shall live by faith" and just as the people of old testament times had to have faith to believe in Jesus Christ for their deliverance and their salvation through Christ; we, too, of today must also do the same and believe in the Lord; Jesus Christ to be delivered from our sins and to be able to live eternally with the Savior once this world has come to its final end.

Hebrews 11:1 says; "Now faith is the substance of things hoped for, the evidence of things not seen." It takes only a little faith for God to make a miracle to transpire. For we must have enough faith to believe then the impossible can be achieved. Reading God's holy word will give us the power that we need to live by faith. Though we weren't there when the actual events took place in the bible to see what really happened; as we read the bible page after page, chapter after chapter, verse-by-verse, line-by-line; God's word comes to life and reveal; what was real.

We, who believe but have not seen the fulfillment of the scriptures in biblical times; are blessed.

For we believe by faith; that Jesus was born of a virgin and was man made flesh, who healed the sick, raised the dead, who died and rose from the grave and who yet lives because he is the Savior of the world. Now, all mankind through him by his grace, his mercy; and the shedding of his blood for the remission of sin; can be saved.

In closing, having faith in God; enables us to climb enormous mountains in our life; towards keeping us on the direct path that leads us to the Savior's safe, loving and warm embrace.

God's love for us is unconditional and it's nothing that we did that's so deserving of it but, it's God's grace that he has for each of us which is God's gift to all mankind. God's love for us is so strong that nothing can separate us from it. No! Nothing and that includes death because even then; God still has love for us.

Back in the historical days; God had a special kind of love for the children of Israel and although the children of Israel sinned, disobeyed God, did evil and rebellious things in the sight of God; he still loved them and had mercy on them. Yet and still; he punished them but he also came to their aid and defense when they would cry out unto him and repent of their sin.

Just as children today are unruly, rebellious, disrespectful and disobedient to their parents; the parent still has to reprimand the children to teach them how to be loving, respectful and obedient human beings to all of God's creation through the love of their teachings.

As a child I was taught about the love of Jesus through a song we sang in church called "Jesus loves me." I often find myself singing this song up out of the blue and it remind me of how much God truly does love me. Even when I may feel that no one in this world really does love me; like I have often felt throughout the years and since the days and the nights of my husband's death. I'd feel lost and alone like no one cares; these precious words of this powerful song would seep out from my lips reassuring me that Jesus loves me and it carried me on; through this maze of life whenever I felt like not wanting to go on in this life. I then, could feel God's love surrounding me as it lifted me and my spirit; knowing that God's love and how he feels about me; is all that really matters to me in this life; which is more than any other love that exist on this earth.

God's love for us is greater than any man's love could ever be or could ever try to compare to make us feel otherwise. For man will lie, cheat and fail us but, God will never lie to us nor will he fail us for his love to us is pure and genuine which will complete us as it fulfills us in this life. God's love stretches far and wide from all sides; and we are completely cover from head to toe by our heavenly Father's love. God's love for us is powerful and real for its agape love from a Spiritual Father who is forever there for us; whenever, we need a shoulder to lean on or to cry on. God's love has no end!

We can't even began to wrap our mind around or about how much God loves each of us. It's immeasurable and untouchable but yet incredible to all who are in need of a loving touch from a loving God. He loves us so much that he sent his only begotten son to die for us and to save us from this sinful world that became corrupt as well as doomed to death. Jesus; the son of God is the only one who can save us and make everything better between God and man.

Jesus chose to do the will of the Father to redeem us through his sacrifice of love for us to die and to shed his blood for us. John 15:13 says; "Greater love hath no man than this, that a man lay down his life for his friends." God loved us first and foremost that he had a plan; to set us free from Satan's evil plot of condemning man and of turning man away from God since the beginning of time.

No one is out of reach to God's love. It does not matter who we are or who we profess to be; God still loves us. It does not matter how rich we may seem to be nor does it matter how poor we are; God loves us. God has more than enough love to go all around the universe. After-all, God made the entire world because of the love that he has for us and absolutely nothing can separate us from his love.

Therefore, we never have to question God's love for us because each day that we awake; is a gift from God for he woke us up with a simple kiss that we could have missed had he not decided to do this. He simply embraced us with a new day and that's more than enough to say how much God loves us; for he didn't have to do it but, he did. God's love is a gift to us and all we have to do is to receive it.

Today, people are so afraid to believe that someone loves them because love is being misused and abused around the world to all age groups; by male or female which doesn't seem to matter at all; whether one may be young or old, black or white, boy or girl, disabled or healthy, an infant or an adult. Abuse is still on the rise today but, we never need to be afraid of God's love for us because it is gentle as an innocent caress.

For one to believe in God's love; there are no strings attached but, the love that this world wants to offer us often comes with a price to pay because some say; "You have to give in order to get."

Some people are preying on the vulnerable and the weak; while lying to them saying that they love them through buying them gifts to try and win them over but, not God. For God's love is free for all and we never have to question or doubt it.

God loves us in spite of what we have done and he loves us in spite of what we may do. We must never feel that we have strayed so far away that he won't accept us back because, God's love stretches far and wide and we never need to run or hide.

Therefore, we must not run from God because, God's love will find us or reach us where ever we may go. People today, will reject us and rub our faults in our face and make us run away but, not God for we are like the lost sheep and God is the good shepherd and he goes out in search of his sheep and brings them safely back to the fold. He will never abandon us or leave us alone.

Meanwhile, we must not wander off; away from the safety zone of God's loving arms that shields and protects us. However, should we happen to fall; God loves us even then and he still will pick us up and help us to stay in the race as he surrounds us with his warm embrace.

We should not take God's love for granted just because we know that God will forgive us and take us back if we fall; rather, we are to strive daily to be more like Christ and to be all that God wants us to be as we love him with all of our heart, mind and strength enjoying his love that he so graciously gives to us daily.

In closing, God's love will be there with us until the end of all time. For his love that he has for us; is easy to find and it's available to all mankind.

Jesus intercedes and stands in the gap for us every day, countless times to God the Father; because the devil constantly wants us destroyed and God sees the blood that his son Jesus shed for us and grants us mercy. God wants us to pray for ourselves as well as others for him to work out the problems in our lives. For we have access to God to intercede for others as Jesus does for us when we humble ourselves in prayer before God.

Many people today do not utilize prayer. Some people may say that they don't know how to pray; while other people may ask the questions: what's the use in praying? Or, what good will praying do? We can start off in prayer to God by acknowledging God and praising God through the Lord's Prayer in Matthew Chapter 6 verse 9. Prayer is simply talking to God with words spoken from the sincerity of the heart that can break down barriers that only God has control of towards making a difference in this world.

Moses prayed for God's mercy on behalf of the children of Israel for their disobedience to God in Exodus Chapter 32 and God spared their lives. Prayer can have great and effective accomplishments when it's according to the will of God because praying and believing by faith is what moves God.

Having corporate prayer is effective as well for we strive to work together in harmony and love expecting God's power from up above to break the chains from the pressure and the temptations of this life through the world; by having total faith in God that he will make a way of escape for all to be able to do so in time of trouble.

However, some things we would like for God to do in our lives will come only through prayer and fasting; meaning that we can't just give God a few seconds of our time and expect everything to be like presto or a snap of the finger. God wants us to cry out to him and meditate and love on him; by thanking him and praising him and partaking of his word instead of indulging in so many earthly food gatherings which takes the place of so many people spending time with him in prayer.

We must pray and fast in order to last against Satan and his deceitful tactics that he has outlined for us. Spending time in the presence of God is what it is going to take for changes to take place; concerning our life on how to stay ahead of the enemy.

Prayer is the gateway to the heart of our heavenly Father; who can open doors and allow miracles to transpire in our lives. There is no need to worry about anything because prayer is a powerful weapon that God wants us to use to defeat the enemy with. We have the power of prayer to help us to rebuke the devil and any forces that come against us in Jesus' name.

Therefore, we must have no fear when calling on the name of the Lord to make our path way clear. The devil trembles at the name of Jesus and the more we call on Jesus, the more fearful the devil becomes and soon he will run in the other direction in which he begun.

1 Thessalonians 5:17 says; "Pray without ceasing." Meaning, we can keep our mind on the Lord and talk to him in prayer anytime, anywhere and no one has to know but God and you. The devil is busy 24/7 and he does his job without cease so why shouldn't we? The enemy doesn't rest from trying desperately to trap or to trip us up..... So, we can't stop our prayer wheel from turning.

Therefore, we must stay in constant prayer always on guard against the evil and demonic forces that are up against us and we will defeat him when we stay in connection with God while going humbly before God.

Meanwhile, we can pray on the job, at home, in the doctor's office, in the courtroom, in class, on the bus, in our car or anywhere we may need to and be in silent communication with God and no one has to know it; but God and you because it will be privately; between you and God.

Hebrews 4:16 says; "Let us therefore come boldly unto the throne of grace, that we may obtain mercy, and find grace to help in time of need.

God loves it when we come before his face in prayer asking him for what we need. But, of course, God does not grant us everything that we may want because, everything isn't always needed and nor is everything that we may want is always good for us.

I think about when my sons were little and about how they would come to me asking for things they wanted or needed and how they came boldly with their request and I would supply them with the need or with what they asked of me. That's how we can approach our heavenly Father through our prayer. God wants us to come to him for whatever it is that we need and if it's according to his will; the need will be supplied.

So, just as a loving father or mother would sometimes do; God denies our request too, sometimes. But, still loves us anyway and we should still love them and be thankful as well as grateful that they are looking out for our best interest at hand. And that they are there in our corner even if they were to say no to us.

Having a talk with God in prayer is wonderful! We can tell God all about our troubles or secrets and no one else has to know. It feels good to be able to ease your mind by spending time in prayer with God.

While the tears run down our cheeks the burden or the weight of it all falls away as God rocks us and eases the pain away at the same time. There is a warmth that comes over us and we began to feel light as a feather; no longer under the weather with sadness but gladness takes over and soothes our heart knowing that God heard our cry as we released whatever it was that troubled us; now we sigh in relief that everything will be alright.

The power of prayer lifts our spirit when we turn everything over to God himself. God is there to help us and he wants to help us but, we must want his help. Therefore, we must go to him and tell him the things that only he can help us with and let God work them out for us.

We must not be afraid to go to God in prayer no matter what the problem may be, for there is nothing that is too hard for God to solve. God has all power and he can do all things and when we really know who God is and how great our God truly is; and to what he can do for us; why would anyone want to hesitate to go to him for anything?

I imagine how I felt whenever my dad would step into the room – Wow!! All eyes and attention was on him and things came to order immediately and that brought smiles to my face to have a dad with such respect as that and he was all mine. Then, I imagine how I felt when my big brother would come on the scene to my rescue whenever someone was trying to push and shove me around. My eyes lit up and I seem to get rough and tough because he was there like a knight in shining armour with me saying to the bully... "Now Whatcha Gonna Do?" So, imagine when God has your back; there's no need to hold back on anything. We can cast all of our cares upon him and he will work it out.

In closing, "Our Father which art in heaven, Hallowed be thy name. Thy kingdom come. Thy will be done in earth, as it is in heaven. Give us this day our daily bread. And forgive us our debts, as we forgive our debtors. And lead us not into temptation, but deliver us from evil: For thine is the kingdom, and the power, and the glory, forever. Amen." Matthew 6:9-13

From a worldly perspective, when one may hear the word ghost, some people may become fearful and think of witches and goblins or so forth. It isn't a subject that many would like to dwell on for a long period of time because some people seem to be frightened of it. However, from a spiritual point of view; the word Holy Ghost can be thought of as supernatural and Godly existence of many wonderful and miraculous things transpiring in a believer's life.

The Holy Ghost gives strength to the believer for difficult tasks to be administered to others about the Lord. The Holy Ghost helps to understand God's word and to discern false teaching by false prophets. It makes intercessors during prayer for the believer one lives a holy lifestyle. The Holy Spirit empowers us to do God's will while it lives within us and helps us to walk righteously and to talk righteously because it is our keeper and our comforter along this straight and narrow pathway that we travel along.

All Saints of God need the Holy Ghost to have that staying power that will lead and guide them into all truth. Just as the Holy Spirit fell upon all flesh during the day of Pentecost; God's spirit is yet being manifested upon his people so that all the world can know that whosoever shall call on the name of the Lord shall be saved.

Every man, woman, boy and girl can receive God's Holy Spirit for it will change their life tremendously so that they will be more like him. Having God's Holy Spirit will give us the boldness needed to carry God's message to others so that they too can then be a bold witness for God to tell others about God; who don't know God.

The Holy Ghost will help us to be presentable towards representing Christ for we must not be ashamed of the gospel. Therefore, he will give us what to say that will be pleasing to him and that will be receivable as well as acceptable to the lost.

After Jesus died and rose; he ministered to his disciples for 40 days and then he ascended up into heaven but he didn't leave his disciples comfortless and neither are his believers today, helpless or hopeless because, the same spirit that led and guided Jesus' disciples; also leads and guides us. God's spirit provides the comfort, peace, joy, love and hope that all believers of Jesus Christ need; to carry out God's plans.

God's gift of the Holy Ghost is given to anyone who is willing to receive him. Without God we can do nothing; for God is the source to all things therefore, we must make him apart of our life to be meaningful as well as plentiful. Just as we need Jesus; we also need the Holy Ghost. Jesus had to go away so that the comforter would come and abide in us and guide us.

The Holy Ghost empowers the believer to be a more effective witness for Christ. It motivates us to get out and get busy for God. God's Holy Spirit lives in us daily and it enables us to be more and more like Christ. The Holy Spirit enlightens us and it instructs us in what to do and what not to do that will help us and not hurt us.

Today in this world; so many people feel lost and alone because they have no one that they can call on. But, if they let God come into their life and fill them with his holy presence; the emptiness will subside on the inside and they will feel alive on the outside. We must choose to deny ourselves from the pleasurable things of this world which causes us to be alienated from God.

We must rely on the Holy Spirit from within us to help us not to become disobedient to God by being selfish and doing fleshly, harmful, devious and evil things. Doing these things makes God angry with us and we therefore, should not provoke God for he is angry with the wicked every day.

We need to depend on the Power of God's Holy Spirit instead of our own power for we can't do this alone; it is too strong for us in our own strength or through the self-conscience mind of our earthly will power that is succumbed by the flesh.

We must be attentive and alert of the evil temptations that are among us and because we are human we are subject to fall to the weakness of our flesh if we are not watchful and prayerful. Therefore, we need spiritual power of the Holy Ghost to intervene and we must allow him to take charge of these fleshly desires that wants to take over our body.

God is a loving and caring Father and he does not want to sit back and see any of his children suffer. Therefore, he forewarns us about destruction that is up ahead and we must take heed and rely on the Holy Ghost to help us in areas of our life that could hurt us or destroy us along the way.

In 1 Kings Chapter 19, Elijah flees for his life and God spoke to him through a still small voice and gave him instructions on what to do while he was in a cave. It does not matter where we are or who we are because God has a way to get our attention. It may be through a raging storm or it may be through a calm, gentle breeze. God still speaks to us; we just have to be attentive and listen to what thus says the Lord; so that we will be able to respond to his call.

Studying God's word helps us to be prepared to witness for God to others. Therefore, we must not ignore or override the Holy Ghost by trying to run from a task that God wants us to do. We can't be afraid to witness to anyone; great or small, rich or poor, black or white, sinner or saint, young or old, married or single, man or woman, boy or girl, near or far, homeless, helpless or hopeless it simply does not matter because it is needed. Therefore, we must be available to do the work of the Lord and not be ashamed of the gospel. The Holy Ghost will teach us all things and bring all things to our remembrance in the hour and time for whoever is in need of a word from the Lord in that moment. We just have to be willing and obedient to do the will of the Lord; to help win souls for God's kingdom.

We have no control over how the Holy Spirit works; for God can use anyone that he chooses to work through for lives to be changed. Just because we may feel that someone is not concerned about changing or living for God; it is not up to us to change them because, it is God who will do the changing. We just may be the one; that God chooses to lead them in the direction in which he is calling them to go in.

Therefore, we must not judge anyone and feel that they are out of God's reach in getting to know Christ because, it's God that woos and wins the heart of people for he knows every one's heart. We just have to play the part that God has placed us in to reach the lost; so that they will be lead to Christ to get to know God and then the Holy Spirit will then live in their heart.

All believers are to be empowered with the Holy Spirit to be able to tell others about salvation. We should not just want to be filled with God's gift of the Holy Ghost by ourselves but, we must want to spread the good news of Jesus Christ to others so that they will want to live a better life that leads them to have eternal life in the end with the risen Lord and coming King in heaven.

In closing, the Holy Spirit is a major role in our life for it empowers us as it transforms us to look like Christ. All believers that are filled with God's Holy Spirit will be changed in the twinkling of an eye; and will be raised up to meet the Lord on judgment day; in the heavenly sky.

Left, Right, Left, Right
Striving forward day and night
Going through ready to fight.

I'm moving along faithfully
And marching on forcefully
Knowing that you're resting on peacefully.

Only God knows my fate
Of my appointed date
While patiently I wait
And of course, I won't be late.

Though I travel through this dreary place
By God's mercy and his grace; as I pick up the pace
Anticipated of seeing my Savior's face.

While listening for the trumpets to sound
I am standing on solid ground and heaven bound
Knowing that one day soon; I will wear my golden crown.

Visualizing the memory of your face
Contemplating the time and the space
Where the moments of the events took place
Knowing that only time can erase.

Only God knows how I truly feel
And my emotions that explains it all is surreal
As I try so hard not to reveal
Wondering how; can I possibly heal?

At times I want to scream
Realizing that this isn't a dream
But, I'd be only blowing off steam
Yeah, I guess that's what it would mean.

But, what good will that possibly do
For I'm still without you
Yes, that's true
Here, yet sad and yet blue.

Only going through the motion
Like being sedated by a potion
From all of the commotion
Wondering what's the notion?

Only on God; I can call
To help me sort it all
No, he won't let me fall
For God will lead me safely through
To one day of being reunited with you.

TODAY

Today, I awoke with a smile
Though I really hadn't slept in a while.

Today, I sat and I sighed
Thanking God today; that I haven't yet cried.

Today, I'm filled with so much hope
Knowing that I can finally cope.

From the pain that was bottled up inside
That I now, no longer have to hide.

Losing you was so dear to me
Now, to understand why; is no longer a mystery.

For today, I can clearly see
That God, meant it to be.

"When you wake up in the morning and you see the sun
Way up in the sky
You know it's not a man that's tall enough
To hang that sun up there
There's got to be a great somebody
To hang that sun up there
Because you didn't do it
And I didn't do it
There's got to be a God Somewhere."

Song By: Mother Jewell R. Morgan

<u>IN LOVING MEMORY OF</u>:
Mother Jewell R. Morgan

ACKNOWLEDGMENTS

I would like to thank my Lord and Savior; Jesus Christ once again through whom all blessings flow for allowing me to be able to do his will of writing and completing this second book with his help. For without his guidance this could not and would not have been possible. I also would like to make mention of <u>my late husband</u>: Marvin Jackson for whom this book was based upon as the true, exemplified solider for God. My partner in Christ; who represented dedication, faithfulness, loyalty, loving and humbleness of service to God as well as to his wife, sons, family and friends. He was my very own personal, "Dr. J." whom I love with all my heart and I thank God for allowing him to be my assigned soldier to cover me. I thank him for his devoted love and support of me that is deeply missed that still flowed through me that helped me not to dismiss this opportunity to complete this assigned mission of publishing this book. We did It J.!!

"IT IS FINISHED!!" And THIS ONE'S FOR YOU!! R.I.P. 'J' – I will see you again my love!!

<u>To my Mother</u>: Mrs. Areatha Beard, whom I love and admire for being a beautiful and loving mother with such grace and meekness but mostly; for being a woman after God's own heart whom I am proud to have and to call my mother! You are God's chosen one for me and no one will ever take your special place in my heart!

<u>To my Son</u>: Tyler Cowser, I thank you for all of your wonderful help in sticking by me to help me on my short comings whenever, I got stuck in areas on my laptop where I needed your assistance to get me back on the right track again (which was quite often). Thank you my son!! I

truly couldn't have made it without you again as usual. I love you beyond measure. For you are my gift from God's very own treasure.

<u>To my Grand-Nephew</u>: Darryl Versery, Jr. (D.J.), you are Auntie's little trooper whom I love so much. Stay humble and loving just the way you are and keep shining brightly like a star. You are dear, you are special but most of all you are loved. Thanks for making me proud to be your aunt.

<u>In Loving Memory of Late Leaders (Soldiers for Christ)</u>: Supt. Elder Joe L. Stocker (Main Street C.O.G.I.C., Elder Lincoln Clardy- Unity Temple C.O.G.I.C.

Elder Odis H. Richmond, Sr. - Tabernacle C.O.G.I.C., Elder Leo Murry- Main Street C. O.G.I.C., Minister Arthur Rodgers- Unity Temple C.O.G.I.C – Thank you all for your words of wisdom and your gudiance throughout the years. Thank you all for being great spiritual leaders to the church family you all are not forgotten. I look forward until that great day in the morning of seeing all of your beautiful smiles again.

<u>In Loving Memory of Late Church Mothers (Warriors for Christ)</u>: Mo. Cleo Johnson, Mo. Willie Mae Brown, Mo. Maggie Tate, Mo. Selma Washington, Mo. Vera Noid, Mo. Harris, Mo. Tidwell, Mo. Murry, Mo. Rosie Haynie, Mo. Mary Mason, First Lady/ Mo. Bessie L. Stocker, Mo. Quince Abercrombie and Mo. Jewell R. Morgan – You all have been great inspirations in my life. I love you all and I look forward to joining you all again someday.

<u>To: Saint Dewitt Hill, Jr.</u> - Pastor of Greater Trinity/Trinity Temple C.O.G.I.C.

<u>To: Elder Willie Farris</u> – First Assembly of God and

<u>To: Elder David O. Jones, Sr.</u> - My Loving Pastor of Kingdom Builders Outreach C.O.G.I.C. - I thank God for each of you being a part of my spiritual upbringing. Your words of God's love and wisdom didn't fall on death ears. May I do justice with God's knowledge of his word that has been etched on my heart from my childhood through my adulthood because of your great teaching and guidance. May God bless you and your family for the love and the kindness that you show

and have shown too many others as well as to myself. Love always, your Sister-in-Christ, Sis. Lynnette Beard-Jackson

To: All of my Loving Present Church Mothers- Mo. Lucy Whitfield, Mo. Doris Holland, Mo. Marjorie Goldsmith, Mo. Versie Cleveland, Mo. Youndle Davis, Mo. Nina Clardy, Mo. Arnita Morris, Mo. Ann Little-Solomon I love you all as though you were my very own real mother. Thank you for the special touch that you give and have given to all young ladies in and out the church. God bless each of you for being chosen representatives of Christ. You are each dear and special to me now and always! You're Daughter-in-Christ, Sis. Lynnette Beard-Jackson

In Loving Memory of My Special Military Soldiers- Mr. Walter Cole, Sr. (Marine), Mr. Anthony Leon Cole, Sr. (Army), Mr. Daniel Taylor, Sr. (Army), Mr. Booker T Jackson (Army), Mr. George Howard,Sr. (Army), Mr. George Howard, Jr. (Army) and to my most dear and special friend Nehamon Lyons IV (Navy)&(Pentagon). Thank God for you all being brave warriors who served for our country. You are each deeply missed and are loved still. Though you are gone from among us; you are certainly not forgotten! To: Wes Leroy, Neil Christopher, Anthony Lim and to my WestBow Press Publishers and staff family thank you for helping me to be able to present another beautiful, packaged, finished product. Thanks for your time invested in helping with my book's beautiful completion. We make a fabulous team!!

Last but definitely not least: To My Spectacular Readers, Family & Friends – God bless each of you once again for sharing in on my success by reading what God has blessed me to write. Your love and your support of me is greatly appreciated and I truly hope that this book will be an extra special blessing to everyone who reads it. Thank you so much for being so special to God and myself that he chose me for this assignment. God bless each of you richly for your support of this book.

Love Always,
Lynnette Beard-Jackson

Printed in the United States
By Bookmasters